英汉对照管理丛书 ⑩

# 人才管理

## TALENT MANAGEMENT
### Pocketbook

【英】安迪·克洛斯 著
（Andy Cross）

菲尔·黑尔斯顿（Phil Hailstone）绘图

张 园 译

上海交通大学出版社
SHANGHAI JIAO TONG UNIVERSITY PRESS

## 内容提要

　　本书为"英汉对照管理丛书"之一,主要介绍了如何在工作中管理人才,包括人才差异、人才网、人才侦查员、人才教练员、人才搅拌器、人才指挥官、人才吸铁石等内容。本书为英汉对照,便于读者在学习管理的同时学到地道的英文表达。

© Andy Cross 2007

This translation of Talent Management Pocketbook first published in 2014 is published by arrangement with Management Pocketbooks Limited

版权合同登记号:图字:09-2013-720 号

### 图书在版编目(CIP)数据

人才管理 /(英)克洛斯(Cross, A.)著;张园译.
—上海:上海交通大学出版社,2015
(英汉对照管理丛书)
ISBN 978-7-313-12430-2

Ⅰ.人... Ⅱ.①克... ②张... Ⅲ.企业管理-人才管理-英、汉
Ⅳ.F272.92

中国版本图书馆 CIP 数据核字(2014)第 292617 号

## 人才管理

| | | | |
|---|---|---|---|
| 著　　者 | [英]安迪·克洛斯 | 译　　者 | 张　园 |
| 出版发行 | 上海交通大学出版社 | 地　　址 | 上海市番禺路 951 号 |
| 邮政编码 | 200030 | 电　　话 | 021-64071208 |
| 出 版 人 | 韩建民 | | |
| 印　　制 | 常熟市文化印刷有限公司 | 经　　销 | 全国新华书店 |
| 开　　本 | 880mm×1230mm 1/32 | 印　　张 | 7.125 |
| 字　　数 | 140 千字 | | |
| 版　　次 | 2015 年 1 月第 1 版 | 印　　次 | 2015 年 1 月第 1 次印刷 |
| 书　　号 | ISBN 978-7-313-12430-2/F | | |
| 定　　价 | 25.00 元 | | |

版权所有 侵权必究
告读者:如发现本书有印装质量问题请与印刷厂质量科联系
联系电话:0512-52219025

## 编辑的话

嗨，大家好！

最早出版这个系列的书（英汉对照管理袖珍手册）是在 2002 年，随后我们又在 2004 年和 2007 年分别推出了第二辑和第三辑。这套丛书（共 50 本）被很多 500 强企业用作培训教材，也被很多读者整套收藏。

这一次，我们对书的开本做了调整。我们给您留出了做笔记的空间。您可以把您查阅的英文单词、词组和句式写在原文下面空白的 Notes 处，也可以把您阅读过程中的所思所想写在此处，把这本书真正变成属于您自己的书。

另外，我们对中文字体也作了调整，让您阅读起来更为轻松。

因为这些调整，书不再那么袖珍，所以丛书名也改为了"英汉对照管理丛书"。

如果您有什么建议和反馈，请别忘了告诉我们！（请发邮件至：wangliatcn@qq.com）

再一次，祝您阅读愉快！

汪 俪

2014 年 12 月

# 目　录

# CONTENTS

# TALENT MANAGEMENT

## 人才管理

TALENT MANAGEMENT

# THANKS FROM THE AUTHOR

I have worked with talented people, in superb organisations, for many years as a leader, recruiter, coach, student and friend. In this book I have included just some of the ideas, beliefs and techniques I have learned and used to help talented people get great results. I love nothing better than watching enthusiastic people achieve more than they ever expected, especially my kids!

My thanks to:

| | | |
|---|---|---|
| Paul Tizzard | Louise Harrison | Moira Nangle |
| Richard Lowe | Sharon Brockway | Sir John Whitmore |
| Frank Dick | Helena Clayton | Adela Cross |

In my work I have read widely and been influenced by many people. There is a list of great books at the back which I thoroughly recommend. My apologies if I haven't accurately referenced where other people have directly influenced what I have written.

*Notes*

_____

_____

_____

_____

_____

人才管理

## 作者致谢

多年来，我在一流的机构中与杰出的人才共事，既是领导、面试官、教练，又是学习者和朋友。我学到了不少帮助优秀人才获得成功的观点、信念和技巧，并将它们付诸实践，这本书涵盖了其中一部分内容。再没有什么比看着满怀热情的人取得超出他们预期的成就更让我欣喜的事情了，特别是我一手培养的年轻人！

我要感谢：

| | | |
|---|---|---|
| 保罗·蒂泽德 | 路易斯·哈里森 | 莫伊拉·南格尔 |
| 理查德·洛 | 沙伦·布罗克韦 | 约翰·惠特莫尔爵士 |
| 弗兰克·迪克 | 海伦娜·克莱顿 | 阿黛拉·克洛斯 |

工作中，我广泛阅读，受到许多人的影响。书后列出了我强烈推荐的好书。若我文中未能准确标注受他人思想直接影响之处，我在此表示歉意。

## TALENT MANAGEMENT

# FOREWORD

## SOME WORDS FROM FRANK DICK, OBE

I've been fortunate to work with some of the most talented people in sport and business. Not everyone will be able to achieve world beating performances, but every one of us can take control of our performance and achieve a little bit higher than we did the day before.

Andy shares my passion for bringing out the potential in people, releasing them to be the best that they can be. I hope that you share this passion too.

This book is a great start point for anyone wanting to better understand how to manage talent. In reading this book you are taking the next step towards being the best you can be, and helping others do the same.

Keep smiling, *Frank*

Coaching has been Frank's raison d'être for decades, inspiring world-beating performances from some of the top names in sport – Daley Thompson, Boris Becker, Gerhard Berger, Denise Lewis, Marat Safin and Katarina Witt. In business, he has helped develop a coaching culture in Barclays, BT, Unilever, Shell, Abbey and Rolls Royce.

*Notes*

_____

_____

_____

_____

_____

# 人才管理

## 前言

### OBE 弗兰克·迪克的一席话

　　我有幸同体育界和商界最富有才华的一些人合作过。不是所有人都能取得举世无双的成就，但所有人都能掌控自己的表现，相比前一天，更进一步。

　　安迪和我一样热衷于挖掘人才潜能，释放他们最大的潜力。希望你也对此报以热情。

　　对任何想要更好地理解人才管理的人而言，这本书是绝佳的起点。读了这本书，你就朝着做最好的自己，及帮助他人做最好的自己又迈进了一步。

　　保持微笑。

　　　　　　　　　　　　　弗兰克

　　弗兰克从事教练一职已数十年，帮助体育界一些顶尖人物取得了骄人的成绩——戴利·汤普森、鲍里斯·贝克、杰哈德·博格、丹尼斯·刘易斯、马拉特·萨芬和卡特尼娜·惠特等。在商界，他帮助巴克莱、英国石油、联合利华、壳牌、阿比和劳斯莱斯发展了教练文化。

# TALENT MANAGEMENT

## INTRODUCTION

Imagine the following:

- ✔ Everyone on your team performs at the highest level every day
- ✔ You are constantly amazed by the no longer hidden talents of your team and their natural desire to perform at their best
- ✔ The best people look for opportunities to work on your team
- ✔ You make good choices so your new recruits blend in quickly with the team
- ✔ People thrive around you and are ready for the next challenge at just the right time
- ✔ When people do move on you can celebrate because they have prepared their own successors
- ✔ Your people leave as advocates for your organisation
- ✔ Some people return to continue their journey with you

**Imagine you are a superb manager of talent.**

Too good to be true? Probably. Something to aim for? Absolutely.

*Notes*

---

# 引言

设想以下情境：

- ✓ 你的所有团队成员每天都以最高水平工作
- ✓ 你的团队成员不再隐藏他们的天赋和发挥最佳水平的本能渴望，经常使你大为吃惊
- ✓ 最出色的人才希望有机会加入你的团队
- ✓ 你慧眼独具，新招收的员工迅速融入团队
- ✓ 你身边的人不断成长，并适时为新的挑战做好准备
- ✓ 员工离职你能送上祝福，因为他已经选好了自己的继任者
- ✓ 你的员工虽然离职，但仍是你的组织的拥护者
- ✓ 一些老员工回到公司继续与你共事

**设想你是位出类拔萃的人才管理者。**

好得不真实？恐怕是。以此为目标？有何不可！

**TALENT MANAGEMENT**

# INTRODUCTION

This book is written for managers and people who support managers, who care about getting results, delivering exceptional products and service, and building sustainable success. Managers who instinctively know that they must pick great people, expect superb results and invest in developing people to be the best that they can be.

Where do you set the bar for yourself?

*Notes*

_____

_____

_____

_____

_____

人才管理

# 引言

　　本书为管理人员所写，也同样适用于那些支持团队领导、致力于取得成效、推出优秀产品和服务、打造持续成功的人。管理人员本能地知道对员工务必择优而取，高要求对待员工，培养人才，让他们发挥出最佳水平。

　　你为自己设定的目标在哪儿？

TALENT MANAGEMENT

# HOW TO USE THIS BOOK

This book introduces the Talent Web: five distinct roles that constitute great talent management (see diagram on page 42). Each role has a 'big' question!

| Role | Big Question |
|---|---|
| **Talent Spotter** | What talent do I need and how can I spot it? |
| **Talent Coach** | How can I bring out the best in my people when it matters most? |
| **Talent Blender** | How can I blend the available talent to get maximum performance? |
| **Talent Conductor** | How can I create a flow of talented people? |
| **Talent Magnet** | What will attract talented people and keep them for longer? |

The book has a section on each role which includes ideas, techniques and beliefs. You may read the book and feel comfortable with what you already do. If so, congratulations; I ask you to share your talent with others. I hope you will find nuggets to improve your own approach. Once you find these, the next step is to prioritise and plan the changes you want to make and enlist the help of others.

You can jump straight into any part of the web. If you do this and get stuck you may need to come back to the start and read the first section on *The Talent Difference*.

*Notes*

人才管理

## 如何使用本书

　　本书介绍了人才网这一概念——构成出色人才管理的五大角色（见 43 页图表）。每一角色面临一个"重大"问题！

| 角色 | 重大问题 |
| --- | --- |
| **人才侦查员** | 我需要什么样的人才，怎么才能发现他们？ |
| **人才教练员** | 我如何能让我的员工在紧要关头发挥出最大潜能？ |
| **人才搅拌器** | 我如何能够融合手头的人才，让他们取得最大的绩效？ |
| **人才指挥官** | 我怎样才能不断创造人才？ |
| **人才吸铁石** | 要靠什么吸引人才，并让他们为我效力更久？ |

　　书中每一角色为一章，包括相关思想、技能和信念。也许你读了这本书后，对自己之前做的工作感觉不错。那么就要恭喜你了，请你与其他人分享自己的才华。希望你能在书中找到有用的信息改善自己的方法。一旦你找到了，下一步就是分清轻重缓急，为自己想做的改变制定计划，并寻求他人的帮助。

　　你可以跳着阅读任一部分。如果你这么做遇到了困难，就需要从头看起，首先阅读第一章人才差异。

# THE TALENT DIFFERENCE

# 人才差异

# THE TALENT DIFFERENCE

## FOCUS ON TALENT

Are you in a 'war for talent' or simply passionate about getting the best from your employees?

This section looks at the case for a greater focus on talent within your organisation.

*Notes*

人才差异

## 关注人才

你是已经身陷"人才争夺战"，还是单纯热衷于让员工发挥最大的绩效？

倘若你任职的机构比较注重人才的话，那么本章讨论的就是这个问题。

# THE TALENT DIFFERENCE

# TALENT HEALTH CHECK

How important is managing talent to your organisation? Answer the following nine questions honestly to identify where a greater focus on talent management could improve your organisation.

| | YES | NO |
|---|---|---|
| 1. Have you found it difficult to fill a key role in the last 12 months? | ○ | ○ |
| 2. Do you rely on external recruits for key roles? | ○ | ○ |
| 3. Do you often compromise on quality at recruitment? | ○ | ○ |
| 4. Have the challenges your team face changed in the last 3-5 years? | ○ | ○ |
| 5. Are you worried that your organisation doesn't have the talent to grow? | ○ | ○ |
| 6. Do your competitors appear to have stronger people than you? | ○ | ○ |
| 7. When people are promoted, are they adequately prepared? | ○ | ○ |
| 8. Do your best people often leave before promotion? | ○ | ○ |
| 9. Are you often disappointed that your people don't achieve what you expected? | ○ | ○ |

## Notes

_____

_____

_____

_____

_____

# 人才差异

## 人才体检

人才管理对你任职的机构而言有多重要？如实回答以下 9 个问题，找出强化人才管理中的哪一点会对你的公司有所裨益。

| | 是 | 否 |
|---|---|---|
| 1. 过去的一年里，你是否难以找到合适的人才填补某一要职？ | ◯ | ◯ |
| 2. 对于关键职位你依赖外部人才招聘吗？ | ◯ | ◯ |
| 3. 招聘时你时常在人才质量上作出让步吗？ | ◯ | ◯ |
| 4. 过去的 3 至 5 年，你的团队面临的困难有变化吗？ | ◯ | ◯ |
| 5. 你是否担心自己任职的机构没有可以培养的人才？ | ◯ | ◯ |
| 6. 竞争对手的人才队伍看上去比你的强吗？ | ◯ | ◯ |
| 7. 升职的人做好充分准备了吗？ | ◯ | ◯ |
| 8. 你手头最好的人才是否经常在升职之前就已离职？ | ◯ | ◯ |
| 9. 你是否经常因员工未能达到你的预期而感到失望？ | ◯ | ◯ |

# THE TALENT DIFFERENCE

## TALENT HEALTH CHECK

Give yourself 1 point for each question you answered positively.

**6 or more**
✔✔✔✔✔✔
Your organisation is likely to either have significant cost or business risk associated with your approach to managing talent

**4 to 6**
✔✔✔✔
Your approach to managing talent is sometimes likely to create frustration and avoidable costs

**3 or less**
✔✔✔
The quality of your people probably gives you an advantage over other organisations; your focus will be needed to keep you ahead

How comfortable are you with the answers for your team or organisation? Which areas concern you the most? What strengths do you have on which to build?

Managing talent effectively must be a priority for any successful manager and business. So, what is the **talent difference**?

*Notes*

# 人才差异

## 人才体检

每答一个"是"得一分。

6 分及以上
☑☑☑☑☑☑     你所任职的机构受你管理人才方式的影响，很可能出现重大损失或业务危机

4 至 6 分
☑☑☑☑     你的人才管理方式有时会让员工灰心或带来本可避免的损失

3 分及以下
☑☑☑     你的团队人才质量相比其他机构更有优势；注意继续保持领先优势

你对自己的团队或机构的答案有多满意？你最关注哪几个方面？你有什么优势可进一步加强？

对于任何成功的管理人员或公司，有效的人才管理必须是重中之重。那么，什么是**人才差异**？

# THE TALENT DIFFERENCE

## WAR FOR TALENT

According to a report produced by two McKinsey consultants in 1998, there is a 'war for talent', a chronic shortage of talent across the board.

| Trends | Impact |
|---|---|
| Increased competition and pace of innovation | Keeping ahead demands the best people |
| Influence of technology | Technology needs brainpower – a talent intensive asset |
| Flatter, leaner organisations | Slower promotions so external moves sought |
| More mergers, acquisitions and outsourcing | Loyalty to a single organisation continues to fade |
| Shrinking 25-45 year old demographics and many senior leaders approaching retirement | Smaller talent pool from which to select |
| Changing attitudes of people towards work | People are more demanding of an organisation to provide meaning, challenge and flexibility |

Good organisations have always employed talented people but recent trends appear to have created a business imperative to focus on finding, developing, using and retaining talent – every manager, every business needs a 'talent mindset'.

*Notes*

人才差异

## 人才战

　　麦肯锡的两位分析师 1998 年发表的一份报告显示，"人才战"已然打响，各个行业都面临着长期的人才短缺。

| 趋势 | 影响 |
| --- | --- |
| 竞争加剧，创新节奏加快 | 保持领先优势需要最顶尖的人才 |
| 技术的影响 | 技术需要脑力——一种人才密集型资产 |
| 更扁平、更精简的机构 | 升职减缓，员工另谋高就 |
| 更多并购和外包 | 对单一机构的忠诚度持续减退 |
| 25~45岁的工作人员数量萎缩，众多高层领导达到退休年龄 | 可供选择的人才减少 |
| 人们对待工作的态度改变 | 员工要求任职机构提供更具价值、更具挑战和弹性的工作 |

　　出色的机构向来聘用优秀的人才，但近期的趋势似乎使得注重人才的挖掘、培养、任用和保留这一工作愈发紧迫——每位管理人员、每个企业都需要"人才思维"。

# THE TALENT DIFFERENCE

## SHORTAGE OF TALENT

Is there really a shortage? Yes, according to most recent research.

An example:

- Average quality of candidates has declined by 10% since 2004
- Average time to fill a vacancy has increased from 37 to 51 days
- 30% of organisations have recruited below average candidates to fill a position quickly

*Corporate Executive Board, 2005, International poll of 4000 hiring managers in 30 companies*

Finding talent is undoubtedly getting harder, but what is the compelling case to manage talent better?

*Notes*

_____

_____

_____

_____

_____

# 人才差异

## 人才短缺

人才真的短缺吗？是的，最近的研究得出的就是这个结论。

例如：

- 自 2004 年以来，应聘者的素质下降了 10%
- 添补空职的平均时长由 37 天升至 51 天
- 30% 的机构为了尽快填补空职，录用水平未达标的应聘者

以上来自 2005 年企业管理委员会（Corporate Executive Board）对全球 30 家公司的 4000 名人事部经理所作的调查

毫无疑问，寻找人才越来越难，可是要把人才管理得更好应该做些什么呢？

# THE TALENT DIFFERENCE

## SHIFTING THE BELL CURVE

Does a talent mindset really make a difference?

It is generally accepted that your best people will increase your operational productivity, profit and sales revenue significantly more than your average performers. Imagine the benefit to your business of shifting the overall performance 'bell curve' to the right.

Research* has shown that a shift in performance from the 50 percentile to the 86.5 percentile will lead to an average increase in financial productivity of 46% in highly complex and professional roles and at least 16% in basic clerical roles.

* Hunter, Schmidt and Judiesch (1990)

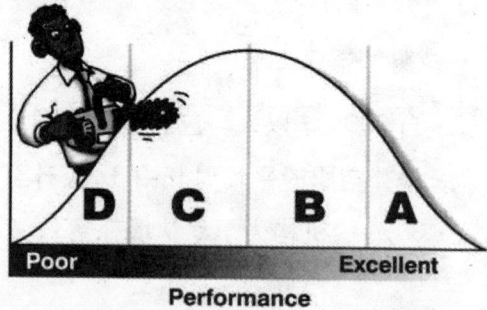

D    C    B    A

Poor                    Excellent

**Performance**

Notes

_____

_____

_____

_____

_____

# 人才差异

## 调整钟形曲线

人才思维当真会起作用吗？

众所周知，顶尖人才比起普通员工会显著增加公司运营的生产率、利润和销售额。设想一下代表员工绩效的"钟形曲线"整体向右移动，你的公司会受益多少？

研究*表明,若员工绩效从第50百分位提升至第86.5百分位,在极为复杂且职业化的岗位会使财务生产率提高46%，在普通的文职岗位则至少提高16%。

\* 亨特,施密特和尤迪施（1990年）

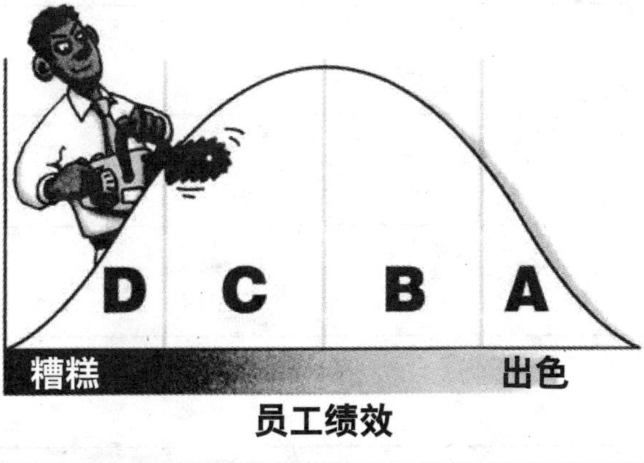

D  C  B  A

糟糕                              出色

**员工绩效**

# THE TALENT DIFFERENCE

## SHIFTING THE BELL CURVE

Some organisations are rigorous in replacing the D's and retaining A's. Other organisations focus effort on defining the traits and attributes of the B's so that they can use this information to recruit more B's and develop the C's.

Some companies view every opportunity to replace someone as an opportunity to upgrade the quality of recruit.

In summary, any effective approach to attract, develop and better use talent has to be a good thing and any improvement in your ability to keep talented people for longer has to benefit the organisation.

Notes

# 人才差异

## 调整钟形曲线

有些机构替换 C 级员工、保留 A 级员工时非常严格。其他机构则侧重分析 B 级员工的特点，以便利用这些信息聘用更多水平达到 B 级的员工，培养 C 级员工。

有些公司总把裁员的机会视为提高新进员工素质的契机。

总而言之，任何有效的吸引、培养和改善人才利用的方法必须不损害他人的利益，你在人才挽留上的任何能力的提高都必须对组织有益。

# THE TALENT DIFFERENCE

## TALENT IS CHANGING TOO!

There are several trends influencing the relationship between the employer and employee:

**Bargaining power**
Company loyalty cannot be assumed: shortage of talent provides greater bargaining power for the best people

**Portfolio career**
Companies are less able to provide long-term security so people see diverse expertise (portfolio careers) as an effective way to reduce risk

**Greater meaning**
People want greater meaning from their work

**Flexibility**
There is increasing desire to *work to live*, rather than *live to work*, and growing interest in more flexible working methods eg times and places

**Fewer boundaries**
Improved technology means that you don't have to be 'at work', or even in the country, to make a contribution

**Informed choice**
People are more aware of their market value and how different employers operate

*Notes*

_____

_____

_____

_____

## 人才差异

## 人才也在变化！

影响雇主与员工关系的几大趋势如下：

### 议价能力
员工对公司的忠诚不再：人才短缺让顶尖人才具备更多议价余地

### 多专长职业生涯
公司越来越不能提供长期的工作保障，于是人们视多样的才能（多专长职业生涯）为降低风险的有效法宝

### 更具意义
人们希望从工作中寻求更多的意义

### 工作弹性
人们更加渴望**为生活而工作**，而不是**为工作而生活**，对富有弹性的工作方式（如工作时间、地点等）更感兴趣

### 界限变少
技术发展意味着你为公司效力时却未必"正在公司工作"，甚至不一定在同一国家

### 知己知彼的抉择
人们更了解自己的市场价值以及雇主们运营方式的差异

## THE TALENT DIFFERENCE

# THE RISK

A war for talent is a risky business; there is a potential 'dark side' to developing a talent elite.

Your best people will, undoubtedly, contribute greatly to your business. However, you may want to consider the following before you embark on any talent agenda:

> *"Fighting the War for Talent is hazardous to your organisation's health...a distraction from what companies should concentrate on... devising systems that get the most out of everyone."*
>
> **Professor Jeffrey Pfeffer**

- Do you value a deep knowledge of your organisation as much as a fresh perspective?
- Will focusing on high-flyers create an undervalued, cynical and demotivated core group?
- Do you define talent to include people outside your senior team – your *hidden* talent?
- Will your attempt to label talent denigrate others?
- Is your approach to talent providing equal opportunity or widening inequalities, eg: race, age, gender and sexual orientation?
- Have you looked at growing your own talent?
- Is your approach benefiting the wider community in which you operate?
- Are you stripping your industry of the most talented people without investing for the future?

*Notes*

_____

_____

_____

_____

_____

# 人才差异

## 风险

人才战是笔有风险的生意：培养精英人才或许有潜在的"阴暗面"。

顶尖的人才无疑会让你的公司业务获益良多。不过，在你开始把人才培养提上日程之前，恐怕要考虑以下几点：

> "打人才战对你的公司危害重重……转移了公司本该用于他处的精力……需建立机制，让所有人发挥自己的最大功效。"
>
> **——杰弗里·普费弗教授**

• 熟悉公司事务和见解新颖在你心目中同样重要吗？

• 关注有可能取得巨大成就的潜力人才是否会让核心团队被低估，成员内心愤愤不平，丧失积极性？

• 你认为人才包括高层团队以外的员工——你的隐性人才吗？

• 你区分人才的举措会挫伤其他员工吗？

• 你的人才管理方式提供了平等的机会还是扩大了不平等，例如：种族、年龄、性别和性取向？

• 你考虑过培养自己的人才吗？

• 你的人才管理方式让你公司所在的社区受益了吗？

• 你抢夺自己行业顶尖人才时是否忘了做长期投资？

# THE TALENT DIFFERENCE

## EQUALITY OF OPPORTUNITY

Most people will accept the need to manage talent if it is coupled with an equality of opportunity, ie giving everyone a fair chance. Some indications that you take the dark side seriously include:

- You invest in people less fortunate outside your organisation
- You look at the future stream of talent (and customers) and provide incentives for people to educate/develop themselves further
- You create jobs and wealth in the groups who support your success

*Notes*

_____

_____

_____

_____

_____

## 人才差异

## 机会公平

　　如果要保证机会均等，即每个人都有同等的机会，大多数人认为人才管理是有必要的。对人才管理的阴暗面有清醒认识的迹象包括：

- 你会为其他机构时运不济的员工花费精力

- 你研究过未来的人才流（和客户流），并鼓励他人自我深造

- 你为支持你取得成功的团队创造就业机会并带来财富

# THE TALENT DIFFERENCE

## WHOLE ORGANISATION

Your focus on talent must go beyond management capability and executive potential; **talent is not restricted to a level or status.** Increasingly, organisations are looking more widely to identify specific areas where there is a strategic business need. A whole organisation approach to talent starts with two questions: what differentiates you from your competitors now? What will keep you in that winning position?

Your answer could be any of the following:
- Great product design
- Exceptional customer service
- Brilliant planning and execution
- Superb sales and distribution
- Above average intellectual property
- Creativity and innovation

Identify your talent focus based on what differentiates your business. Once you know where to start, agree the unique abilities that will drive success and the specific issues you face. You can then segment your approach to talent and create your own map – now you know where to invest your efforts.

*Notes*

## 人才差异

## 全局战略

对人才的关注不能停留于管理能力和执行潜力；**人才并不局限于某一水平或地位**。越来越多的机构放宽眼界，挖掘存在战略业务需求的特定领域。对整个公司进行人才培养首先要回答两个问题：你与竞争对手不同在哪儿？你保持竞争优势的法宝是什么？

你的答案可能包括以下任意几点：

- 出色的产品设计
- 突出的客户服务
- 卓越的计划和执行
- 一流的销售与分销
- 平均水平以上的知识产权
- 创造力与创新力

公司人才管理的重心取决于公司业务的独到之处。一旦你理清头绪，就要认可自己取得成功的独特能力，并确定你面临的特定问题。然后，你便可划分人才管理方式，制定自己的人才管理地图——现在你知道该从哪儿下功夫了。

# THE TALENT DIFFERENCE

## ANSWERING THE CYNIC

Some managers may want to bury their heads in the sand and ignore the debate. You may hit blockers, particularly when talking about developing your own talent in preference to recruiting externally.

**Cynic: Why fuss about growing your own talent?**

There is a world of talent out there and some of them already work for you! HR may deal with the impact of losing your best people and the cost of replacing them **but it is a business risk.** Don't get complacent; remember to treat your current staff with at least as much respect as people who have yet to prove themselves in your organisation.

**Cynic: But our best people always want more money**

Yes, and they will also want greater challenges, more recognition, exposure to your senior managers and for you to show a genuine interest in their future. If you are a skilled talent coach your investment will pay dividends.

*Notes*

_____

_____

_____

_____

_____

## 人才差异

### 应对玩世不恭者

　　某些管理人员可能想逃避现实，忽略这个争议。你或许会遭遇一些阻力，尤其是当你谈到比起外部招聘更优先考虑从内部培养人才的时候。

**玩世不恭者：何必在培养自己的人才问题上小题大作？**

　　人才多如牛毛，而其中有些人已经在为你效劳了！人力资源部可以处理顶尖人才流失的冲击，应对替换他们的成本，**但这是一种商业风险**。别自我感觉太好；记住，要尊重手头的员工，至少把他们当做尚未在你的机构中崭露头角的人来对待。

**玩世不恭者：最顶尖的人才总想要更多钱**

　　没错，他们还想要更大的挑战，更多的认可，以及在你们高级管理人员面前露脸的机会，这样你才会真正关心他们的未来。如果你掌握了人才教练的技巧，你的投资会得到回报的。

## THE TALENT DIFFERENCE

# ANSWERING THE CYNIC

**Cynic: And then they walk out the door**

If you manage your talented people well they will stay longer and more than repay the time and effort you have invested in them. Your challenge is to act like a talent magnet, get everyone making a difference and keep the best for longer.

**Cynic: Why worry; talented people will always rise to the top anyway**

Possibly, but will it be in your organisation? As a talent coach you have a role to create a talent flow and make sure your people arrive at the next stage well prepared and quicker. If you leave it to chance, raw talent may stay raw!

**Cynic: I've already got the best people so I'm OK**

There is always someone more talented on your tail – you never have the winning formula for long. You need to be able to stay ahead, which means being creative enough to do today, what others will do tomorrow.

*Notes*

_____

_____

_____

_____

_____

人才差异

## 应对玩世不恭者

**玩世不恭者：之后他们就拍屁股走人了**

如果你管理人才得当，他们会跟随你更长时间，给你的回报绝不止你曾经在他们身上投入的时间和精力。你的挑战在于做一块人才吸铁石，让每个人发挥功效，把最出色的人才留得更久。

**玩世不恭者：为什么要担心；有天赋的人不管怎样都能自己爬到高处**

或许吧，但在你的机构里可能吗？作为一位人才教练，你的职责是不断创造人才，确保员工晋级时不仅胸有成竹而且用时更短。如果你听天由命的话，璞玉依然还是璞玉！

**玩世不恭者：我已经有最顶尖的人才了，所以我无所谓**

总有比你更出色的人才尾随你身后——你不可能永远都是赢家。你需要保持优势，这就意味着要创意十足，今天就做别人明天才会做的事。

THE TALENT WEB

人才网

# THE TALENT WEB

## FIVE LINKED ROLES

Still reading? Do you recognise the talent difference and the contribution it will make to your business? Are you curious about your role in managing talent?

The rest of this book is based on the talent web – five linked roles that you need if you are to excel in this area.

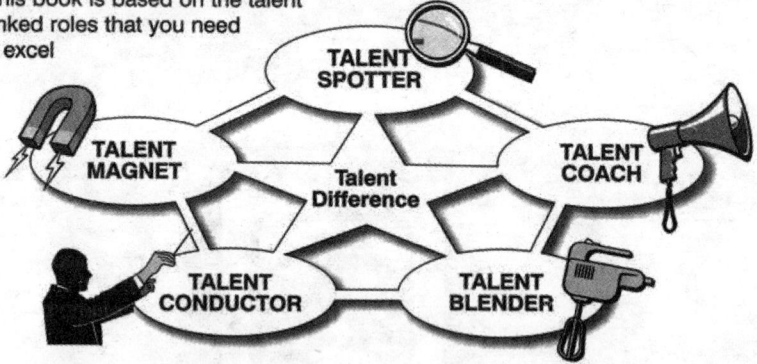

TALENT SPOTTER

TALENT MAGNET

TALENT COACH

Talent Difference

TALENT CONDUCTOR

TALENT BLENDER

*Notes*

_____

_____

_____

_____

_____

## 五大关联角色

　　你还在看么？你认识到人才的差异和对你的企业的贡献了吗？你好奇自己在人才管理中的角色是什么吗？

　　这本书接下来的内容建立在人才网上——你若想在人才管理方面出类拔萃，需要了解五大关联角色。

# THE TALENT WEB

# FIVE LINKED ROLES

I've used the web analogy for several reasons:

- Each strand of the web is as strong as steel and incredibly sticky but has even more power when all the strands pull together
- Putting the first thread in place relies heavily on luck and the wind; after that each one can be quickly strengthened
- Incredible effort is needed to build the web but its reusability and ability to deliver make it a fantastic investment
- The web transmits vibrations through every strand to let you know it is working

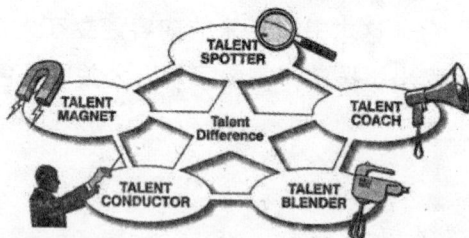

*Notes*

_____

_____

_____

_____

_____

人才网

## 五大关联角色

我用网络来做类比的原因在于：

• 网络中的每一条线既坚固如钢，又相互粘连难以分割，当它们拧成一股时会更强大

• 第一条线的到位多半靠运气和时机；之后各条线会很快巩固

• 建成网络需要下大力气，但它可以反复使用，实现起来完全有可能，是一笔绝妙的投资

• 网络通过各条线传递共鸣让你知道它正在运行之中

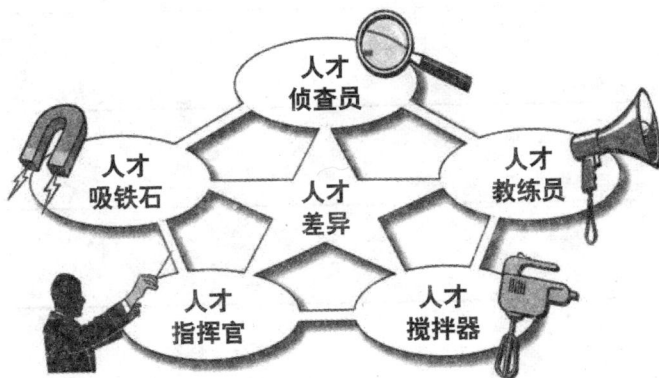

# THE TALENT WEB

## THE BIG QUESTIONS

Each role in the talent web has its very own 'big' question.

| Role | Big Question |
|------|-------------|
| Talent Spotter | What talent do I need and how can I spot it? |
| Talent Coach | How can I bring out the best in my people when it matters most? |
| Talent Blender | How can I blend the available talent to get maximum performance? |
| Talent Conductor | How can I create a flow of talented people? |
| Talent Magnet | What will attract talented people and keep them for longer? |

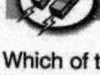

Which of these questions can you answer now?
Which ones would you identify as priorities for you to answer?

## Notes

_____

_____

_____

_____

_____

人才网

# 重大问题

人才网中的每一角色都有自己的"重大"问题。

| 角色 | 重大问题 |
|---|---|

**人才侦查员** — 我需要什么样的人才,又怎么能找到他们?

**人才教练员** — 我怎么让我手下的员工在紧要关头发挥出最大潜能?

**人才搅拌器** — 我如何能够融合手头的人才,让他们取得最大的绩效?

**人才指挥官** — 怎样才能不断创造人才?

**人才吸铁石** — 什么能够吸引人才,并让他们为我效力更长久?

这些问题你目前能回答哪几个?

你认为哪几个问题需要优先回答?

# 人才侦查员

人才
侦查员

才石

人才
差异

人教

What talent do I need and how can I spot it?

**我需要什么样的人才，又怎么能找到他们?**

## TALENT SPOTTER

# DEFINITION

If you are going to make the most of your talented people you have to be able to recognise talent in the first place – you have to be a talent spotter. So, what does the word mean? Look for a definition using Google and you will get the following:

| | |
|---:|:---|
| *Main entry* : | Talent |
| *Part of speech* : | Noun |
| *Definition* : | Ability |
| *Synonyms* : | Aptitude, aptness, art, capability, cleverness, command, flair, genius, gift, inventiveness, knack, know-how, mastery, power, savvy, skill, strength |

1. A person who possesses unusual innate ability in some field or activity
2. Natural endowment or ability of a superior quality
3. A variable unit of weight and money used in ancient Greece, Rome and the Middle East. A talent of gold was double the weight of a talent of silver

*Notes*

# 人才侦查员

## 定义

　　如果你想让自己手头的人才发挥出最大的功效，你首先得识别人才——你得做一位人才侦查员。那么，"人才"这个词是什么意思？用谷歌搜索定义，结果如下：

| | |
|---|---|
| **主词条**：人才 |
| **词　性**：名词 |
| **定　义**：能力 |
| **同义词**：天资、聪慧、本领、能力、机灵、掌控力、天分、天才、天赋、创造力、窍门、诀窍、精通、力量、常识、技巧、优势 |

1. 在某一领域或行为上有超常天赋能力的人
2. 天生拥有的优良品性
3. 古希腊、古罗马和中东地区使用的可变的重量和货币单位。金泰伦 (talent) 的重量是银泰伦的两倍。

## TALENT SPOTTER

# BEING THE BEST YOU CAN BE

What do you look for when you are talent spotting? Ability, yes, but ability alone won't lead to enduring success. As they grow, even talented people need to have the courage to succeed or fail, to learn how to respond to defeat and how to bounce back. Sometimes talented people find life too easy and don't learn the lessons they need to succeed.

**What qualities would be top of your list?**

1st Passion to achieve
2nd Determination and perseverance
3rd Curiosity to learn and change
4th Ability

**These translate into tough questions you should ask your team and yourself:**

1. Do you want to succeed?
2. Do you believe you can succeed?
3. Will you keep going until you get there?

There are always people with more ability. The challenge for each individual is to have the passion, determination and curiosity to be the best **they** can be!

*Notes*

_____

_____

_____

_____

_____

人才侦查员

## 做最好的自己

　　你在探查人才的时候寻求的是什么？能力，是的，不过单单靠能力不可能一直成功。在成长的过程中，即便是有天赋的人也需要有面对成功或失败的勇气，学习如何应对失败，如何重新振作。有些时候优秀的人才会觉得日子过得太轻松，没得到成功所需的历练。

**哪些品质是你最看重的?**
第一　取得成就的激情
第二　决心和毅力
第三　学习和变革的好奇心
第四　能力

**把这些品质转换成你需要询问团队成员和你自己的尖刻问题：**
1. 你想要成功吗？
2. 你相信你能成功吗？
3. 你能坚持到底直至成功吗？

　　总有比你更有能力的人。一个人面临的挑战是保持激情、决心和好奇心，做最好的自己!

## TALENT SPOTTER

# MINDSET

One of the most important factors when spotting talent is mindset, those people who go that little bit extra when it really matters. Frank Dick describes people as either Mountain or Valley people. Pay attention to what people say, what they do and how they respond to a challenge and you will soon know if you have a Mountain person on your hands!

**Valley People**

- Seek calm and comfortable ground and shelter
- Value safety and security
- Aim 'not to lose' so playing for a draw is OK
- Are fit to survive but little else
- Make excuses for not acting and believe others have all the luck

*Notes*

_____

_____

_____

_____

_____

# 人才侦查员

## 心态

搜寻人才时最重要的关注因素之一是心态，需要的是那些关键时刻会多走一小步的人。弗兰克·迪克将人分成峰型和谷型两类。注意员工说了什么，做了什么，又是如何应对挑战的，这样你很快就知道自己手头的员工是不是峰型。

### 谷型人群

- 追求安逸的环境和居所
- 注重安全和保障
- 目标是"不输"，所以平局也很好
- 适合生存，但别无其他长处
- 为自己的不作为找借口，觉得别人都比自己幸运

## TALENT SPOTTER

# MINDSET

### Mountain People

- Take the risk of winning because there is no such thing as the risk of losing
- Aim to be the best they can
- Take personal accountability for their own performance
- Want to test ambition on the toughest climbs
- Will fight and endure discomfort to overcome difficulties

Adapted from *Winning: Motivation for Business, Sport and Life*, Frank Dick OBE

*"You have to lean away from the mountain if you're going to learn to ski."*

Anon

 *Notes*

_____

_____

_____

_____

_____

## 心态

### 峰型人群

- 为成功冒风险，因为没有为失败冒风险这种事
- 立志发挥自己最好的水平
- 对自己的表现负责
- 想通过最艰难的攀爬考验自己的雄心
- 为了克服困难，会奋力拼搏并忍耐不适

改编自《胜利：生意、运动和生活的动力》（*Winning: Motivation for Business, Sport and Life*），OBE 弗兰克·迪克著

"要学会滑雪就得把身体往山的反方向倾侧。"
——Anon

**TALENT SPOTTER**

# APPRECIATE YOUR TALENT

Everyone has talent but some hide it better than others. A healthy organisation will provide the opportunity for **every employee** to be the best that they can be.
Do you appreciate all of the talent in your organisation?

Within the scope of your team's ambitions, objectives and expectations, how do you define talent? Try this activity to start to define talent in your organisation:

Get together a cross-section of your employees, including senior managers, and ask the following appreciative questions:

1. Our best people can be described as....
2. The magic in our people usually shines when....
3. We are most successful in our organisation when...
4. Our future success depends on people who.....

Use the list you create or review your existing definitions of talent and agree what you must keep doing to find the talent you need.

*Notes*

人才侦查员

## 赏识自己手下的人才

人人都有才华，只是有些人藏得比别人更好罢了。一个健全的机构会为**每一位员工**提供机会，让他们做最好的自己。你欣赏自己组织里的每一位人才吗？

在你的团队的志向、目标和期望的范围内，你是怎么定义人才的？尝试下面这个活动，着手为你任职的机构定义什么是人才：

找来一组不同部门的员工，包括高级管理人员，问以下带有倾向性的问题：

1. 我们最好的员工是……样的
2. ……的时候，我们的员工会焕发自己的神奇力量
3. ……的时候，我们在自己任职的机构中最成功
4. 我们未来的成功取决于……样的人

用你列出的清单来定义人才或重新审视自己已有的人才定义，明确你找寻需要的人才时必须要做的工作。

## TALENT SPOTTER

# IDENTIFYING TALENT

Where do you set the bar when defining talent? Is it the people who stand out from the crowd? The people with a genius for making things happen? The following definition builds on ability and includes the dimension of **impact** on you and others.

Talent is:

- A genius for making things happen...
- With a minimum fuss...
- Inspiring others to do the same

**Low**

| | |
|---|---|
| **BACKBONE** Gets on with the job in hand. Unlikely to set the world alight or drive change | **REAL DEAL** Gets results and drives positive change. Has a positive impact on others |
| **MISTAKE** Is a drain on your time, your headcount and your customers | **PRIMA DONNA** The dilemma. Exceptional performance at a cost to the overall team and you |

Maintenance

**High**

Impact

Low　　　　　　High

Talent is often associated with *prima donna* behaviour – explosive and attention-seeking but undeniably able to make a significant difference. The performances must be good enough to justify inclusion. Don't fall into the trap of assuming that the most visible and vocal people are the most talented.

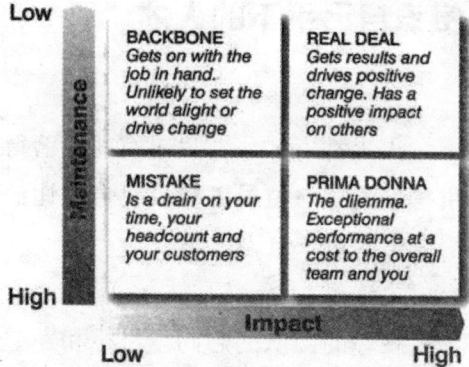

_Notes_

_____

_____

_____

_____

_____

# 人才侦查员

## 辨识人才

你定义人才的时候把标杆设定在哪儿？是特别显眼的人？还是特别擅长落实任务的人？以下的定义以能力为基准，兼顾其对你和他人的影响程度：

人才：

• 特别擅长落实任务…

• 遇事沉着冷静……

• 激励别人向他看齐

人才经常会被认为有点恃才傲物——有争议性、高调，但无疑能起到重大的作用。必须表现极好才能被归入这类人群。不要掉入圈套，以为最高调的人是最有天赋的。

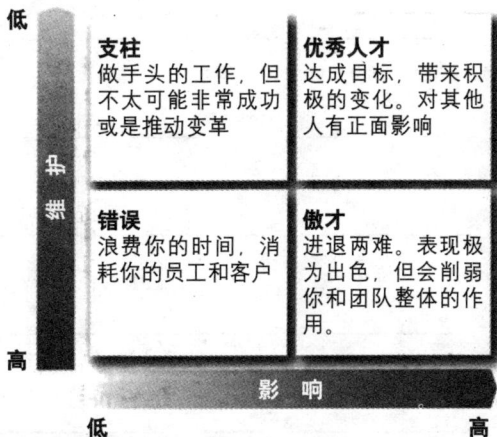

低

高

**支柱**
做手头的工作，但不太可能非常成功或是推动变革

**优秀人才**
达成目标，带来积极的变化。对其他人有正面影响

护
无

**错误**
浪费你的时间，消耗你的员工和客户

**傲才**
进退两难。表现极为出色，但会削弱你和团队整体的作用。

影 响

低　　　　　　　　　高

**TALENT SPOTTER**

# FLYING START

What does it take to get raw talent off to a flying start? Investing your time early pays dividends but do be careful not to stifle talented people. A fresh perspective doesn't last forever and being too directive and controlling can make it disappear even quicker. The best you can do for your new people is to give them opportunities to meet people and understand the business, ask them questions and provide constructive feedback.

1.   Hold up the mirror – raise self-awareness by providing high quality feedback. A simple approach like **AID** usually works wonders:

**A** ction            What you have observed

**I** mpact            The implications of the action

**D** esired Outcome   What needs to be done next time

Remember the AID model can be used to frame positive feedback, with the 'Desired Outcome' being: **do it again!**

*Notes*

人才侦查员

## 快速成长

想让未经训练的人才快速成长需要做些什么工作？尽早投入时间会起效果，不过要注意别扼杀人才。新鲜的点子不会源源不断，控制欲太强会让这样的想法消失得更快。给新人以机会结识他人，了解业务，问他们一些问题并给予一些建设性的反馈，你能做的至多也就是这样的工作。

1. 高举镜子——提供高质量的反馈，提高员工的自我意识。像 **AID** 这样简单的方法往往能收到奇效：

**A**ction （行动）                         你观察到了什么

**I**mpact （影响）                         行动的内在含义

**D**esired Outcome （期望的结果）    下次需要做什么

记住，AID 模式可以用来表达正面反馈，"期望的结果"可能是 **再做一遍!**

**TALENT SPOTTER**

# FLYING START

2. Help people **GROW** – ask questions that encourage improved performance:

**G** oals       What are you trying to achieve?

**R** eality      What's happening now?

**O** ptions     What could you do?

**W** hat        What are you actually going to do?

3. Get them clued up – organise a route map for the individual to find out how the organisation operates, the complexities of the industry and the customer and/or product experience.

*Notes*

_____

_____

_____

_____

_____

## 快速成长

2. 帮助员工**成长（GROW）**——问一些促进员工进步的问题：

**G**oals （行动）　　　　　你想取得什么成绩？

**R**eality （现实）　　　　现在是什么情况？

**O**ptions （选择）　　　　你能做什么？

**W**hat （什么）　　　　　你打算做什么？

3. 让他们熟悉业务——为每个人画一张路线图，让他们了解机构的运行方式，行业的复杂性以及顾客和（或）产品体验。

# TALENT CHAMPIONS

Every organisation has talent champions – the people who excel at finding hidden talent and helping them thrive. Who are yours?

**Cheerleaders** — Excellent at pushing people into the limelight and getting recognition for those with potential

**Bridge Builders** — Have the magical ability to open doors, build bridges and, most importantly, connect talented people with key decision makers

**Guardian Angels** — Can put up a protective umbrella so that people can act with some freedom, and experiment in relative safety

**Wise Owls** — The people with organisational know-how and awareness, who help others avoid conflict, understand the politics and navigate around the business

How do you personally champion talented people?

> *"There is something much more scarce, something rarer than ability. It is the ability to recognise ability."*
>
> Robert Half

*Notes*

_____

_____

_____

_____

_____

人才侦查员

## 人才管理能手

　　每个机构都有人才管理能手——特别善于挖掘潜在人才并帮助他们茁壮成长的人。你机构里的是谁？

**拉拉队长**　　擅长把他人推到台前，能辨别出有潜力的人

**搭桥人**　　有打开大门、构筑桥梁的魔力，最重要的是，能让有才华的人与做关键决策的人搭上线

**守护天使**　　打开保护伞让他人较为自由地行动，并在较为安全的环境下做出尝试

**智慧猫头鹰**　　具备组织技能和组织意识的人，帮助他人规避冲突，理解组织政治，一心扑在业务上

　　你个人是怎么支持有才华的人的？

> "有一种东西比能力更为稀缺、更为珍贵。这便是识别能力的能力。"
> ——**罗伯特·霍尔**

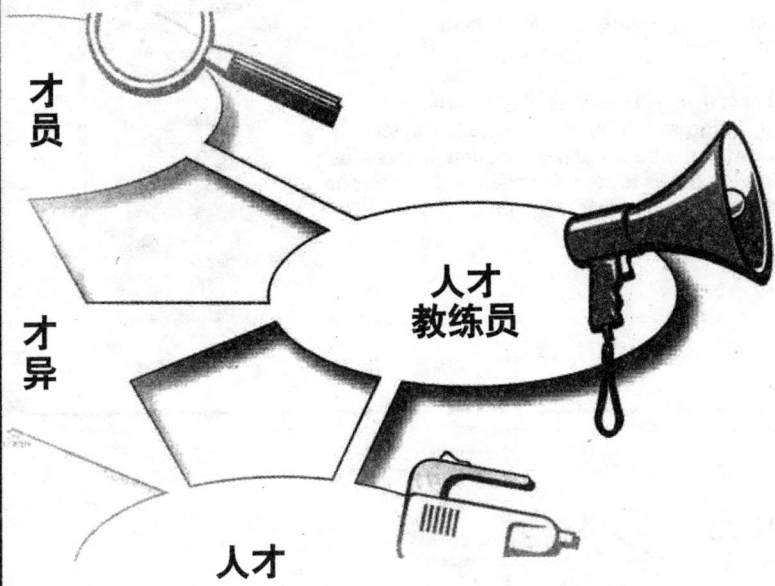

才员

才异

人才

人才
教练员

# 人才教练员

*How can I bring out the best in my people when it matters most?*

**我怎么让我手下的员工在紧要关头发挥出最大潜能?**

## TALENT COACH

# HARNESSING THE POWER OF TALENT

What mindset do you have when you manage your people?

People often describe talent as needing to be harnessed or channelled.

If you view talent as a river, your role as a talent coach is to channel the water; acting as the banks to guide the water downstream; narrowing the banks at the right time to increase the pace; widening the banks to slow the pace and encourage reflection...but never letting the river stagnate.

> *"If managing retention in the past was akin to tending a dam, today it is more like managing a river. The objective is not to stop the water from flowing but to control its direction and speed."*
>
> **Peter Cappelli**

## Notes

_____

_____

_____

_____

_____

## 人才教练员

## 利用人才的力量

你做人才管理的时候是怎么想的？

人们常把人才理解为需要加以利用和指引的人。

如果你把人才视为河流，那么你作为人才教练员的工作就是驭水；如河岸一般把水流导向下游；适时收窄河岸，加快水的流速；拓宽河岸放缓流速，以便产生回流……但绝不能让河流变成死水。

> "如果过去储留人才类似大坝的维护，那么如今它更像治河。目的不是阻挡水的流动，而是控制它流动的方向和速度。"
>
> ——彼得·卡佩利

## TALENT COACH

# LESSONS FROM JACK WELCH

Jack Welch was Chief Executive of General Electric for many years, having climbed successfully through the ranks. His beliefs about the role of leadership in developing talent within the business have brought General Electric to the forefront of talent management. Here are some of the lessons all good talent coaches need to learn:

1. **Relax** (and manage less) – stop getting in people's way and looking over their shoulders. Let people perform and you will be surprised at the results.

2. **Instil confidence** – treat people with respect and build confidence in others so they keep things simple.

3. **Think boundary-less** – encourage ideas at all levels and act on them. Get your talent searching for new ideas inside and outside the organisation.

4. **Encourage the stretch** – push for the impossible and encourage people to go beyond ordinary goals. If the goals are not reached, fine, as long as people have truly tried.

5. **Infectious enthusiasm** – for you and all those around you, your customer must always be your passion.

Adapted from *29 Leadership Secrets from Jack Welch*, by Robert Slater

## *Notes*

_____

_____

_____

_____

_____

人才教练员

## 从杰克·韦尔奇身上学到的经验

杰克·韦尔奇担任通用电气公司的首席执行官多年，成功地通过一级级职位爬上高位。他对领导层在企业培养人才方面发挥的作用的看法，让通用电气走到了人才管理的前沿。这里有些优秀的人才教练员必学的经验：

1. **放松**（减少管理）——不要插手，不要背后监视。让员工自己表现，你会对取得的成果大吃一惊。

2. **注入信心**——尊重员工，助其建立自信，这样他们才不会把事情复杂化。

3. **不为想法设限**——鼓励各级员工开动脑筋并付诸实践。让你手头的人才在机构内外找寻新点子。

4. **鼓励延伸**——敦促员工尝试难以达成的任务，鼓励他们超越寻常的目标。如果没有达成目标，没关系，只要他们认真尝试过就好。

5. **热情待人**——不管是对你还是对你身边的人来说，客户必须始终是你最热情相待的人。

*改编自《杰克·韦尔奇的 29 个领导秘诀》，罗伯特·史雷特著*

TALENT COACH

# WISH FOR WHAT YOU WANT
## EXPECTATIONS set BELIEF sets REALITY

It's a simple equation.

What you believe matters. **If you limit your belief in others then you limit their potential.** Nine times out of ten, people limit their own performance because of low self-belief. Your best performers will have a strong self-belief underpinned by technical competence. That 'knowing feeling' in their own abilities means they will consistently exceed expectations. You have a role in developing self-belief in others.

EXPECTATIONS set BELIEF sets REALITY

*Notes*

人才教练员

## 说出自己的期望

**期望使信任成为现实**

这是个简单的公式。

信任很重要。**如果你保留自己对他人的信任，那么你就限制了他们的潜力。**十次有九次，我们因为不够自信而限制了自己的表现。你手头最顶尖的人才会因专业能力过硬而非常自信。他们那种对自己能力的"知晓感"意味着他们会不断超越预期。你的工作职责之一是培养他人的自信。

期望使信任成为现实

## TALENT COACH

# WISH FOR WHAT YOU WANT

As a talent coach, consciously raising what you expect of others can enhance their performance:

- Encourage your people to set high personal standards
- Always expect the best – stop when you hear yourself doubting others
- Be positive and stay positive – let others know when they start to use negative language
- When performance dips, help people bounce back quickly by expecting a superb performance next time; focus on what went well (especially since talented people are naturally self-critical)
- Ask people what they believe is possible, building on the passion, and help them to describe the practical steps to achieve the dream

## Notes

_____

_____

_____

_____

_____

人才教练员

## 说出自己的期望

作为一位人才教练员，下意识地提高你对他人的期望会改善他们的表现：

• 鼓励你的员工为自己设立高标准

• 永远期待最好的结果——一旦你发现自己在怀疑其他人，赶紧打住

• 始终保持积极的心态——当别人开始言语消极的时候，让他们意识到这一点

• 绩效下滑的时候，表明对员工下次出色表现的期待，帮助他们快速振作；把注意力放在做得好的地方（这点特别需要，因为人才天生就具有自我批评的意识）

• 询问员工他们相信什么是凭热情可以做到的，并帮助他们描述实际可行的措施以达成梦想

TALENT COACH

# THREE TYPES OF GOALS

A manager will help talented people set goals. A great coach will help people set the **right type** of goal and understand the difference. There are three types of goals which alone have little impact but come alive when you bring them together.

**Outcome Goals** – dreams, inspiring or ambitious end goals
**Performance Goals** – milestones, targets, progress goals
**Process Goals** – technique, quality goals

People need dreams to which to aspire. A great coach will help people describe their dreams and stretch what is possible. They will then break these dreams into a series of performance milestones that, if achieved, will make the dreams come true. Progress is rarely in a straight line so the coach will help talent keep focused on the motivating outcome. The coach will also encourage people to focus on the key technical aspects of performance that will deliver a quality performance.

*Notes*

_____

_____

_____

_____

_____

人才教练员

# 三种目标

　　管理者会帮助人才设定目标。而一位出色的人才教练员会帮助他们设定**合适的**目标，并了解两者之间的差异。这里有三种类型的目标，孤立存在时没有太大的作用，可一旦结合使用便会焕发活力。

　　**结果目标**——梦想，鼓舞人心、雄心勃勃的目标
　　**业绩目标**——里程碑、指标、进步目标
　　**过程目标**——技巧、质量目标

　　人们需要梦想作为奋斗的目标。一位出色的人才教练员会帮助员工描绘他们的梦想，并全神贯注于可能实现的梦想。然后，他们把这些梦想划分成若干业绩里程碑，达成这些里程碑，也就实现了梦想。进步往往不会一帆风顺，因此人才教练员要帮助人才把注意力集中在激发他们斗志的成果上。教练员同样要鼓励员工注重业绩关键的技术性方面，这样才能实现高质量的业绩。

# SETTING THE BAR

Talented people will naturally aspire to be the best they can be, but everyone needs a little support to set the bar in the ideal place. The following checklist will help you teach others how to set the bar.

### 1. COMMITMENT

- Get people to list the goals they want to achieve
- Writing down and sharing goals can help create momentum and build commitment
- Encourage them to focus on three to four priorities (the business world often expects complex and multiple goals)

### 2. UNDERSTANDING

- Ask your people to explain the goals to you
- Listen for the emotions that will explain the underlying motivation – use this knowledge to coach people should energy reduce
- Help differentiate between the types of goals (see previous page)
- Encourage people to be precise and realistic in setting goals

*Notes*

_____

_____

_____

_____

人才教练员

# 设定目标

有才华的人自然而然地会想把事情做得最好，但每个人都需要一点支持，来把目标定在理想的位置。以下清单在你教别人设定目标时可以派上用场。

### 1. 承诺

- 让员工列出自己想要达到的目标
- 写下目标并分享目标有助于获得动力，建立承诺
- 鼓励他们优先关注三至四个项目（商界经常期望达成复杂且复合的目标）

### 2. 理解

- 让你的员工向你解释他们的目标
- 倾听了解员工的情绪，因为情绪暗示着动机——对员工进行教练时利用这点知识往往能事半功倍
- 帮助员工区分不同类型的目标（见前页）
- 鼓励员工设定精确且现实的目标

## TALENT COACH

# SETTING THE BAR

### 3. PLANNING

- Start to build the plan together
- Work backwards to break each goal into achievable chunks
- Identify tests, controls and measures that will let you track the milestones that matter most
- If they get off track help them learn and adjust the plan
- Encourage measurement against the best inside and outside the organisation, rather than against people less able

### 4. SUPPORTING

- Agree your coaching role
- Agree the personal support you will provide
- Identify doors you may need to unlock and hurdles you are well placed to overcome
- Agree when you will revisit the goals and measure progress (make it within six weeks)

*Notes*

人才教练员

# 设定目标

### 3. 制订计划

• 一起着手制订计划

• 回头把每一个目标划分成可能实现的小块

• 制订考核方法、进度掌控方式和衡量标准，这样可以帮助你追踪最重要的几个里程碑

• 如果他们偏离了目标，要帮助他们认识到这一点并调整计划

• 制定的衡量标准要针对机构内外最优秀的人才，而不是水平较低的人

### 4. 支持工作

• 认可自己的教练身份

• 确定自己可以提供的个人支持

• 找到你需要打开的大门，以及以你的身份方便克服的障碍

• 确定你回顾目标进程和考核进度的时间（最好在 6 周以内）

# PREPARING PEOPLE FOR CHANGE

The negative impact of poorly managed change within organisations can be huge. If change gets a big fanfare, but little else, it's a recipe for failure that can lead to discomfort and resistance. We all know about the change curve and it is your role to help flatten the curve and accelerate the pace through which people achieve acceptance. Then you can start to focus on performance!

> "Excellence is an art won by training and habituation. We are what we repeatedly do. Excellence, then, is not an act but a habit."
> Aristotle

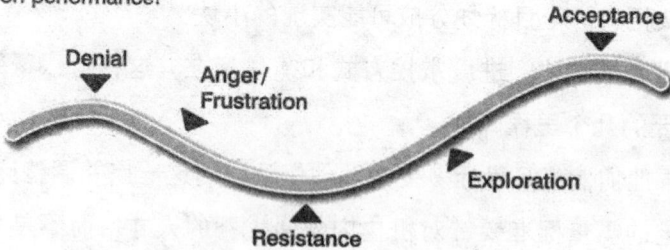

Denial

Anger/ Frustration

Acceptance

Exploration

Resistance

---

Notes

_____

_____

_____

_____

_____

## 让员工为变革做好准备

在一个机构中，变革处理不当带来的负面影响巨大。如果支持变革的呼声很高，但别无其他表现，这就是失败的迹象，可能引发不满和抵触情绪。我们都知道变革曲线，你的职责就是让曲线

"卓越是一门通过训练和惯例造就的艺术。我们反复做什么，就会成什么样的人。因此，卓越不是一种行为，而是一种习惯。"
——**亚里士多德**

变得平滑，让员工尽快接受变革。这样你才能着手关注绩效！

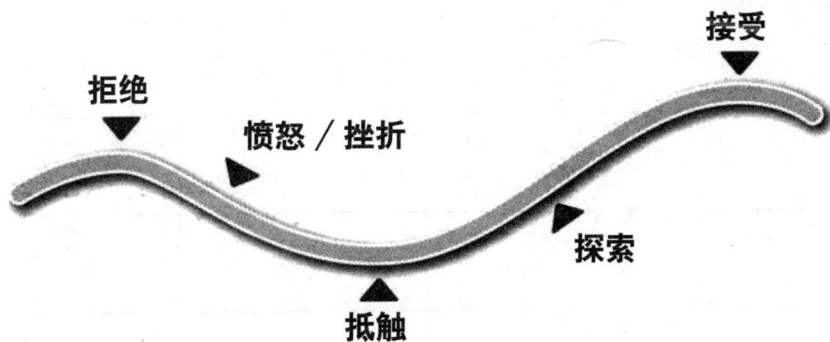

拒绝

愤怒／挫折

接受

探索

抵触

## TALENT COACH

# PREPARING PEOPLE FOR CHANGE

It is important to describe the future destination – the end result of the change. It is also important that you work with people **to plan the journey,** to set realistic targets, provide feedback and help people get back on track when they stray off line.

> *"The harder I practice and work at my game the luckier I get."*
> Gary Player, golfer

Yes, it is important that people can learn the behaviours and techniques necessary for future success. It is more important that you create the opportunity for people to practise under pressure and in different environments.

A great coach will prepare talented people for change, instil the importance of practice and coach them through the change.

**Skill = Technique under Pressure**

A spectator can talk a great game.
A player has the ability to perform.
A talent has the skill to perform under pressure.

*Notes*

---

人才教练员

## 让员工为变革做好准备

描绘未来的终点（变革的最终结果）非常重要。同样重要的是你和员工一同**规划这段旅程**，设定现实的目标，提供反馈，在员工迷失方向时帮助他们返回正轨。

没错，员工学习未来成功之路上所需掌握的行为和技巧非常重要。更为重要的是你能为员工创造机会，在不同的环境下负压训练。

一位优秀的教练员会让人才为变革做好准备，向他们灌输实践的重要性，并在整个变革的过程中辅佐他们。

> "我训练越努力，对比赛越专注，运气就越好。"
> ——加里·普莱耶，高尔夫选手

### 技能 = 压力下的技巧

观众可以对一场精彩的比赛评头论足。

球员能上场比赛。

人才可以在压力下表现良好。

## TALENT COACH

# THE JOURNEY

One of my favourite analogies for coaching people is the journey.
The more challenging the journey, the more skilled you need to
be as a coach. Add your own ideas to the themes below:

**Destination**
You have to be able to describe the destination in a way that inspires
others. Paint a picture of a better place – a compelling vision!

**Clear Path**
How well have you described the route? How easy will it be for
others to follow or even guide you? How will you know that you
are still on the path? If it gets dark, who will shine the light so
you can see the way ahead?

**Preparation**
How will you get people ready for the journey? What planning,
preparation and fitness will increase the likelihood of success?
Do they need passports?

*Notes*

_____

_____

_____

_____

_____

人才教练员

# 旅程

我最喜欢把对人员的教练比作旅程。旅程越艰难，你作为教练就需要越老练。为以下的主题加入自己的想法：

### 目的地
你得把目的地描绘得让人向往。画一个更美的地方——引人入胜的图景！

### 明确的路线
你把路线描绘得有多好？其他人跟随你或是指引你容易吗？你怎么知道自己走对了路？若是天黑了，谁会点亮你前方的道路？

### 准备
你怎么让员工为旅程做好准备？哪些计划、准备和训练会提高成功的可能性？他们需要护照吗？

## TALENT COACH

# THE JOURNEY

### Energy
How will you generate the energy and motivation to make others want to follow? How will you sustain that energy during the journey and who will provide the energy when you are not around? How quickly will you travel?

### Arrival
How will you adjust your path if your destination changes or the path becomes an impasse? How will you know when you have arrived? What have you learned from the journey?

### Onward Journey
How will you ensure that you have the energy to take on the next challenge, which could simply be getting down the mountain?

 *Notes*

_____

_____

_____

_____

_____

人才教练员

# 旅程

### 能量

你怎么产生能量和动力，让别人自愿跟随你？你怎么在旅途中维持那份能量，你不在时又由谁来提供这份能量呢？你旅行的速度如何？

### 抵达

如果目的地改变了，或者路线堵塞，你会怎么调整路线？你怎么知道你已经抵达目的地了？你从旅行中学到了什么？

### 继续前行

你怎么确保自己还有能量接受下一个挑战，即便这个挑战可能像下山那么简单？

# STRENGTH BASED DEVELOPMENT

Many development activities are based on traditional *gap analysis* where people are assessed against either an unrealistic expectation, eg perfection, or worse still against average. The resulting development plan seeks to address shortfalls.

A more realistic and positive approach is to accept some weaknesses will be difficult to improve and at best will be managed. This allows you to **focus on developing strengths and improving areas with potential.** In other words, build your greens, strengthen your ambers and manage around your reds.

**Development traffic lights**

Accept and manage

Develop

Talk about, build and use

Notes

_____

_____

_____

_____

_____

人才教练员

## 强项训练

许多培养活动是在传统的差距分析的基础上进行的。评估者不是将被评估者与不可企及的期望值，比如完美的表现相比较，就是将其与平均水平相比较，这个更糟。结果就是，制定的培养计划着重弥合期待值与现实情况的差距。

更为现实和积极的方法是接受事实——某些弱点很难提高，至多也就是能够控制。这样你便可以**专注于发展强项，改善有进步潜力的地方**。也就是说，发展绿灯，加强黄灯，管理好红灯。

### 人才培养交通信号灯

## TALENT COACH

# STRENGTH BASED DEVELOPMENT

With the development traffic lights in mind you can use the following to have a more constructive development conversation:

- Identify and fully discuss *green* strengths – spend time emphasising the areas they are best at and build self-esteem (so they'll accept tougher feedback later)
- Build on or more fully develop strengths to compensate for weaknesses, eg being an excellent coach means you can get the best from creative people, even if you are not creative yourself
- Provide opportunities for these strengths to be used within your business, eg look for projects that need great change managers
- Identify *amber* opportunities that are important either to role or aspirations and put in place development activities
- Agree *red* weaknesses and plan how best to avoid or manage around these

*Notes*

_____

_____

_____

_____

_____

人才教练员

## 强项训练

把人才培养信号灯铭记于心，你便可以用以下方法展开建设性的培养谈话：

• 辨别出绿灯强项并充分探讨——花时间强调他们最擅长的领域，培养自尊心（这样他们以后就能接受较为严厉的反馈）

• 通过加强或充分培养强项来弥补弱点，比如，作为一位优秀的教练员，你可以充分挖掘创造性人才的潜能，即便你自己并不是很有创造力

• 在你的业务中提供利用这些强项的机会，比如，寻找需要优秀变革管理者的项目

• 辨别出重要的黄灯机会，不论是对人还是对工作，把培养活动落到实处

• 明确红灯弱点，制定计划规避或管理好这些弱点

# STIMULATE CREATIVITY

**What do you do to stimulate your best people?**

If you don't trust your people you naturally limit both performance and creativity – why would they want to take the risks necessary to excel? Many managers will take the safe option when managing others and over-control the detail, leading to short-sighted answers. If you effectively treat your employees as an extra pair of hands they will do little more than you ask.

It's also human nature for people to assume that certain rules exist, eg *I have to sit at my desk; everyone else does and no-one has told me that I can go for a walk*. Creativity is about being different from the crowd, in how you think and how you act.

*Notes*

_____

_____

_____

_____

_____

人才教练员

## 激发创造力

你怎么激励自己手头最优秀的人才？

如果你不信任自己的手下，自然会限制住他们的表现和创意——他们为什么要去承受那些为了胜过他人必须冒的风险？许多管理人员在管理他人的时候往往都很保守，而且太过把握细节，最终的成果便显得目光短浅。如果你把你的员工当作额外的帮手，他们所做的事情很少会超出你要求他们做的。

人本能地觉得有某些潜在规则，比如，我得坐在桌前；其他人都坐着，没人告诉我可以出去走走。创造力就是打破常规，不论是想法上还是行动上。

**TALENT COACH**

# STIMULATING ENVIRONMENT

What can you do to provide a more stimulating environment?

Encourage people to:
- Challenge the barriers to when work takes place, eg time and location
- Question the process
- Have fun!
- Relax and slow down – that's when the sparks fly
- Break habits and get uncomfortable for a while
- Have direct contact with people
- Book time to think into the diary
- Read, travel and walk around

What three things could you do to increase your own energy at work? Ask your talented people the same question.

*Notes*

_____

_____

_____

_____

人才教练员

## 激发创意的环境

你怎样才能提供一个更能激发创意的环境呢?

鼓励员工:

- 对工作上的障碍提出异议,比如时间和地点
- 质疑工作的流程
- 找乐子!
- 放轻松并放缓速度——这时才会创意火花满天飞
- 打破常规,忍受一阵子的不适
- 与其他人直接交流
- 预留时间想想自己一天都做了什么
- 读书、旅行、溜达

做哪三样事能增强你工作的干劲?也用同样的问题去问你手头的人才。

**TALENT COACH**

# WHY COACHING WORKS

Coaching focuses on how people can develop and implement their own ideas and practical solutions – translating goals into action. It is about increasing personal responsibility and encouraging people to take ownership of the issues, the very traits that differentiate talented people from others.

There are many coaching models and most have similar stages to those listed here:

### Goals into action

| STAGE | AIM |
|-------|-----|
| Identify issues | Awareness and interest |
| Set goals | Responsibility |
| Generate options | Discovery |
| Agree boundaries | Ownership and consistency |
| Understand power | Freedom and interdependence |
| Review success | Learning |
| Take action | Performance |

Find yourself a coaching model you feel comfortable with and use it – every day!

*Notes*

## 为什么教练有用

教练的主要工作是让员工拓展自己的想法和实际的解决方案，并将其付诸实践——把目标转化成行动。重点在于提升个人责任感，强化员工对待问题的主人翁意识，这些正是人才有别于其他人的特质。

教练人才的模式有很多，但它们大多都有和下面列出的内容相似的阶段：

**目标变行动**

| 阶段 | 目的 |
|------|------|
| 明确问题 | 意识和兴趣 |
| 设定目标 | 责任 |
| 产生选项 | 发现 |
| 明确界限 | 归属权和一致性 |
| 理解权力 | 自由和相互依赖 |
| 回顾成功 | 学习 |
| 采取行动 | 绩效 |

自己找一个你觉得好用的教练模式使用——每天如此！

## TALENT COACH

# UNDERPERFORMANCE

Even your best people can be stopped in their tracks by complacent management. When your talent doesn't perform, use this checklist to identify what action, within your control, will make the difference.

1. Task clarity — Do they know what *good* looks like?

2. Task priority — Do they understand the impact of what they are doing?

3. Competence — Do they have the skills to do the job?

4. Obstacles — What are the real or imagined procedural barriers (rules) that are getting in the way?

5. Reward for failure — Are your decisions rewarding the wrong behaviour?

6. Performance feedback — Are you providing consistent and timely feedback on how they are doing?

7. Role/Person mismatch — Have you put them in the right job or team?

8. OK, they are being wilful! — Let people know the consequences

## Notes

_____

_____

_____

_____

_____

## 人才教练员

## 绩效不佳

即便是最出色的人才也会因为漠不关心的管理而停滞不前。当你手头的人才工作没有进展时，使用以下列表，看看在你职权范围内采取什么措施会起效果。

1. 明确任务　　　　他们知道什么叫"好"的表现吗？

2. 优先任务　　　　他们知道自己正在做的事所带来的影响吗？

3. 能力　　　　　　他们有做这份工作的技能吗？

4. 阻碍　　　　　　哪些实际的或设想的程序上的障碍（规定）在挡道？

5. 失败的奖励　　　你的决策在奖励错误的行为吗？

6. 绩效反馈　　　　你对员工的表现有连贯且及时的反馈吗？

7. 职责／人员不匹配　你把他们安置在合适的位置或团队中了吗？

8. 好吧，他们就是故意的！　让员工知道这么做的后果

## TALENT COACH

# MOVING TOWARDS SUCCESS

At a basic level, people's motivation to perform can be described as either 'towards' or 'away from', ie they are motivated to generate or to avoid a particular emotion. For example, one person may work hard to prepare a presentation because they enjoy the 'buzz' of people valuing their contribution. Another person may prepare equally well for the same presentation to avoid appearing ill-informed.

Listen carefully to your people (a common theme in this book) and you should be able to spot the underlying motivation, the strength of the emotion and whether it is a positive force. As a talent coach you should encourage:

1. A positive 'towards' articulation of the motivation – a healthier place to start.

2. Alignment of team and individual goals with the main motivational drivers.

3. Reflection on achievements; putting into words how success feels helps people to understand themselves better. They can then 'bottle' the emotion for use when they next need a boost.

*Notes*

人才教练员

## 迈向成功

员工工作的动机基本上可以说或者是想"接近"什么，或者是想"避开"什么，比如，他们想引发或是避免某种情绪。举个例子，一位员工认真准备报告是因为他享受众人讨论他作出的贡献时"闹哄哄"的样子，而另一位同样认真地准备报告是为了避免让自己显得消息不灵通。

认真聆听员工的想法（这是本书的主题），这样你就能察觉出他们潜在的动机，情绪强烈不强烈，动机是否正面，等等。作为一位人才教练员，你应该鼓励：

1. 员工阐明自己想"接近"什么的动机——一个较为健康的出发点。

2. 通过主要动机驱动协调团队与个人的目标。

3. 反思成果，阐明成就感如何帮助员工更好地了解自己。这样，他们就可以暂时"瓶装"自己的情绪，等待下一次需要动力的时候使用。

# SPITZER'S EIGHT DESIRES OF MOTIVATION

Everyone is motivated differently so it is vital that you know what makes your best people tick. A skilled manager will take every opportunity to hit the motivational 'hot buttons' of their people. Spitzer identified eight different motivators for individuals.

**Power**
Motivated by status, control of their future and opportunities to progress.

**Activity**
Motivated by interest and variety in their work.

**Recognition**
Needs praise and to be acknowledged for good work, and given guidance when they go wrong.

**Affiliation**
Motivated by social contact, friendship and team spirit.

**Competence**
Likes to use their strengths, address their weaknesses and learn from mistakes.

**Ownership**
Needs to get involved and be part of decisions that affect their job.

**Meaning**
Needs to feel that they have a definite role in the team and a positive contribution to make, gaining a sense of worth from their work.

**Achievement**
Needs to feel challenged and developed at work, with realistic goals to achieve.

*Notes*

人才教练员

## 施皮策的八大动力欲望

　　每个人的动力都不同，因而你必须了解驱动你手头最优秀员工的是什么。老练的管理人员会把握每一次机会，击中员工动机的"热点"。施皮策发现了八大个人动力。

**权力**
由地位、对未来的掌控力和进步机遇驱动。

**活动**
由兴趣和工作的多变性驱动。

**认可**
表现好时需要表扬和认可，做错事时需要指引。

**归属感**
由社交、友谊和团队精神驱动。

**能力**
喜欢发挥自己的长处，提升自己的劣势，从错误中吸取经验。

**主人翁精神**
需要参与对自己工作有影响的决策，积极加入其中。

**意义**
需要知道自己在团队中有明确的角色，可以做出积极的贡献，并且可以从工作中获得价值感。

**成就**
工作时需要挑战和进步，并有现实的目标可以实现。

# SPITZER'S EIGHT DESIRES OF MOTIVATION

You may know your people well enough to identify their two or three key motivators. If not, or if you wish to help them better understand their own drivers, then try this exercise.

### Step 1
Ask them to write on Post-it notes 10 things that really excite and motivate them.

### Step 2
Ask them to associate the items on their list with the eight desires.

### Step 3
Ask them to identify which ones feature most often and decide on their two or three main motivators.

### Step 4
Ask them to identify elements of their current role which satisfy the key motivators and what could be done differently to increase their motivation.

| Name | Justine | Julie | Jamal |
|---|---|---|---|
| Power | ✔ | | |
| Recognition | ✔ | ✔ | ✔ |
| Competence | | | ✔ |
| Meaning | ✔ | | |
| Activity | | ✔ | |
| Affiliation | | ✔ | |
| Ownership | | | |
| Achievement | | | ✔ |

*Please tick which motivators you believe apply to your staff – how can you use this information better to coach them?*

# Notes

_____

_____

_____

_____

_____

人才教练员

# 施皮策的八大动力欲望

也许你对自己的员工很了解，能察觉出两到三个他们的关键动力。如果并非如此，或是你希望帮助他们更好地了解自己的驱动力，那么就试试下面这个练习。

### 步骤 1
让他们在便利贴上写下 10 样最令他们激动、最能激励他们的东西。

### 步骤 2
让他们把列出的条目和八大欲望挂上钩。

### 步骤 3
让他们选出最经常起作用的几个条目，选择两到三个主要动力。

| 姓名 | 贾丝廷 | 朱莉 | 贾马尔 |
|---|---|---|---|
| 权力 | ✔ | | |
| 认可 | ✔ | ✔ | ✔ |
| 能力 | | | ✔ |
| 意义 | ✔ | | |
| 活动 | | ✔ | |
| 归属感 | | ✔ | |
| 主人翁精神 | | | |
| 成就 | | | ✔ |

请勾出你认为适用于你的员工的动力——你怎么利用这些信息来更好地对他们进行教练？

### 步骤 4
让他们找出当前职位上契合关键动力的元素，以及还可以采取哪些措施来增强他们的动力。

**TALENT COACH**

# GROWING A COACHING RELATIONSHIP

Coaching is never a static relationship and, in reality, movement is exactly what you should be aiming towards. Frank Dick talks about the coaching relationship changing over time as the individual grows in self-belief and self-awareness.

| Phase | Relationship |
|-------|-------------|
| Accepting | Coach says, *'this is what you do'*. |
| Exploring | Individual starts to ask questions to understand. Coach shares thinking. |
| Challenge | Individual has drive and ambition to make well-expressed and timely challenge. Coach listens and responds positively. |
| Winner | Individual has strong emotions about performance and result. Coach challenges. |
| Champion | Individual wishes to leave a legacy. |
| Legend | Individual wants to be remembered for the quality of winning. |

Do you have confidence in your own ability to let the relationship grow?
Do you know when to pass the coaching relationship on to someone better placed?

*Notes*

_____

_____

_____

_____

_____

# 人才教练员

## 发展教练关系

教练从来不是一种静态的关系，其实你的目标应该是建立动态的关系。随着时间的推移，员工的自信和自我意识不断增强，教练关系也会不断变化，弗兰克·迪克就此谈了自己的想法。

| 阶段 | 关系 |
| --- | --- |
| 接纳 | 教练员说：'这就是你该做的。' |
| 探索 | 员工为了了解情况开始提问。教练员分享自己的看法。 |
| 质疑 | 员工有动力有雄心，会及时提出质疑，把自己的想法表达到位。教练员聆听后作出积极回应。 |
| 胜者 | 员工对于工作的表现和成果情绪激烈。教练员提出异议。 |
| 冠军 | 员工想脱离旧体制。 |
| 传奇 | 员工希望因常胜而名留青史。 |

你对自己发展教练关系的能力有信心吗？

你知道该在什么时候把教练员的身份传递给更合适的人吗？

TALENT COACH

# WORK LIFE BALANCE

Talented staff can limit their long-term performance and value to the business, and damage their health by running out of positive energy owing to a lack of work life balance. They can become obsessed with achieving results at work – regardless of anything else! This can have a negative and destructive impact on other areas of their lives.

Talent managers who are excellent at coaching for work life balance:

- Discuss life outside work to give a picture of their lives 'in the round'
- Identify passion and interests outside the workplace
- Adapt work to fit lifestyle issues
- Ensure their talented staff only work late on an exceptional basis
- Set a good example by not working late too often themselves
- Encourage and review achievement of goals inside and outside work

*Notes*

人才教练员

## 兼顾工作和生活

　　有才华的员工会因为缺乏对工作和生活的平衡而限制自己在公司中的长远表现和价值，耗尽正能量后也会损害自己的健康。他们可能会变得过分在意工作的结果——完全不考虑其他东西！这可能会对他们生命中的其他领域带来负面甚至毁灭性的影响。

　　擅长教练员工兼顾工作和生活的人才管理者：

- 会谈论工作之外的生活，"360 度"地描绘自己的生活

- 发现职场之外的兴趣爱好

- 调整工作来适应生活方式问题

- 确保有才华的员工只是因为特殊情况才加班

- 以身作则，不过多加班

- 鼓励员工工作内外都设定并实现目标，并对其进行检查

## TALENT COACH

# WORK LIFE BALANCE

Talent managers are also quick to spot the early triggers of talented staff with poor work life balance:

- Consistently working late
- Accepting more work than they can healthily manage
- Looking increasingly tired or unhealthy
- Losing their patience or becoming unusually irritated

*Provided by Richard Lowe*

# Notes

_____

_____

_____

_____

_____

# 人才教练员

## 兼顾工作和生活

当有才华的员工工作和生活失衡时，人才管理者能及时发现早期征兆：

- 长期加班
- 接受自己能力之外的工作量
- 看上去越来越疲惫和不适
- 失去耐心或变得莫名暴躁

由 Richard Lowe 提供

## TALENT COACH

# MENTORING

Coaching is a powerful management style to adopt with talented people. However, the personal change that the individual may go through as a result means that he or she may also need to find a suitable mentor.

So, what is the difference?

| Coaching | Mentoring |
| --- | --- |
| Zoom lens/close up | Wide angle lens |
| Results | Values and vision |
| Performance | Potential |
| Short-term | Long-term |
| Focused on detail | Change in perspective |
| Specific | Eclectic |
| Gets you to find answers | Provides advice on shortcuts |

*Notes*

_____

_____

_____

_____

_____

# 人才教练员

## 辅导

教练是一种适用于人才的有效管理方式。不过，教练后员工会经历个人改变，这就意味着他们可能需要找到一位合适的导师。

那么，教练员和导师的差别在哪儿呢？

| 教练 | 辅导 |
| --- | --- |
| 变焦镜头，密切关注 | 广角镜头 |
| 成果 | 价值观和远见 |
| 绩效 | 潜力 |
| 短期 | 长期 |
| 注重细节 | 看法的改变 |
| 具体的 | 不拘一格 |
| 助你找到答案 | 为走捷径出点子 |

# TESTING HIGH PERFORMERS

How your best people respond when challenged with extra work is a relatively strong indicator of potential.

In his book *'The Peter Principle'*, Dr Laurence J Peter describes the effect when a person with strong technical ability gets promoted, based solely on performance, to a management position and fails. The different mindset required in the management role means that the new job doesn't suit the individual.

Can you plot each of your people using the circles below? The final two describe visually how a high performer may respond to the challenge of additional responsibilities. The final picture is what you would expect with true talent and readiness.

**Not yet full performance**

**Full performance**

**Inappropriate response**

**Exceptional performance**

*Notes*

---

---

---

---

---

## 测试高绩效的员工

最优秀的人才对额外工作的应对处理可以很好地反映他们的潜力。

在《彼得原理》这本书中,劳伦斯·J·彼得描述了这样一个效应,就是当一个专业技术能力很强的人因表现出色升到管理职位后往往会干得不好。管理角色需要不同的理念,这说明新的职位并不适合这个人。

你可以用下面的圆圈来绘制员工的表现吗?可以看出,最后两张图描绘了表现出色的员工对额外任务的应对。最后一张图描绘的才是真正有真才实学且能胜任工作的人会有的表现。

   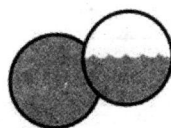

**未充分表现**　　　**充分表现**　　　**反应不当**　　　**表现出色**

**TALENT COACH**

# POSITIVE ROLE MODELS

A great deal of informal learning is as a result of good and bad role models. To help your best people tap into this learning, encourage them to watch others carefully and take the time to reflect on what they see, hear and feel.

Try this exercise. Think about the most memorable and impressive colleague you have known. Name them and identify:

1. What really made them remarkable and memorable?
2. Which of their exceptional strengths had nothing to do with intelligence?
3. What impact did each strength have on you?
4. In what ways did you think or act differently as a result of your contact with them?

If you are not able to find a positive role model you can, of course, complete this exercise based on a bad role model (what not to do!).

*Notes*

人才教练员

## 正面范例

　　正面或负面的范例会带来很多潜移默化的学习。为了帮助你最出色的员工利用好这种学习，需要鼓励他们认真观察他人，花些时间反思他们的所见所闻和所感。

　　试试这个测试。回想你认识的同事中让你最难忘、印象最深刻的人，说出他们的名字然后找出：

1. 他们出色在哪儿，为什么能让你记住？
2. 他们的哪些长处和智力没有关系？
3. 每一长处对你的影响如何？
4. 你和他们接触后在思想和行为上有了哪些改变？

　　如果你找不到一位正面的范例，你当然还可以用一个负面典型来完成这个测试（别做什么！）。

## TALENT COACH

# QUESTIONS FOR TALENTED PEOPLE

An effective approach to managing performance should mean that your people can answer the following questions at any time.

**Key questions for review time or when priorities change, eg new role or project**

- What are my objectives and how do these contribute to the team objectives?
- What is the stretch for me and the business?
- What support do I need to be successful?
- How can I learn and develop from opportunity?
- How will I know I have been successful and how often will I check I am on track?

**Key questions for regular 1-2-1s**

- What have I achieved and is this what I promised?
- What didn't get done? What would get me back on track or provide greater stretch?
- How have priorities changed?
- What knowledge or skills do I need to refresh/develop to achieve my objectives?
- Overall, how well am I meeting expectations?

*Notes*

_____

_____

_____

_____

_____

人才教练员

# 为人才准备的问题

有效的绩效管理意味着你的员工可以随时回答下面的问题。

**做总结或优先事项改变时（比如新的职位或项目）的主要问题**

- 我的目标是什么，它们对团队目标有什么贡献？
- 我和公司的方向在哪儿？
- 我要成功需要哪些支持？
- 我如何从机遇中学习和进步？
- 我怎么知道自己已经成功，我多久会检视一次自己是否仍在正轨？

**一对一讨论时的主要问题**

- 我取得了什么成绩，是我承诺做到的吗？
- 什么没做到？什么能让我回到正轨，或给我提供更好的路线？
- 优先事项发生了怎样的变化？
- 我需要重拾或加强什么知识技能来达成我的目标？
- 总体来说，我在达成预期目标方面做得怎么样？

人才
教练员

人才
差异

才官

人才
搅拌器

# 人才搅拌器

How can I blend the available talent to get maximum performance?

我如何能够融合手头的人才,让他们取得最大的绩效?

**TALENT BLENDER**

# INGREDIENTS FOR A TALENTED TEAM

1. First check the ingredients you already have in the cupboard.
2. Then add quality to the pot, using the best affordable ingredients.
3. Stir the pot and watch carefully as the team raise their game and success attracts others.

*Notes*

_____

_____

_____

_____

_____

# 人才搅拌器

## 人才团队所需的原料

1. 首先检查自己碗橱里已有的原料。
2. 然后用你用得起的最好的原料来提升品质。
3. 搅拌锅子，认真观察，团队在工作中不断提升，他们的成功会吸引其他人。

**TALENT BLENDER**

# INGREDIENTS FOR A TALENTED TEAM
**FIVE TIPS**

Check that you have the following:

1. The necessary technical experts in your team – you must be able to deliver your core product and service.

2. A common purpose and understanding within the team of the challenge ahead – talented people are passionate about challenge. This is best looked at as a team so that everyone understands their own contribution, what others will contribute, and they can see a visible shared commitment.

3. Complementary rather than similar personality attributes. While diversity may seem like a more difficult option, the difference and conflict it can create are far more likely to lead to breakthrough performance for your team – it just needs a talented manager.

4. A genuine desire amongst your talented people to help others achieve. They need to work hard and care about the team's results, not just their own.

5. People you feel you can trust – this could be people you have worked with before.

_Notes_

# 人才搅拌器

## 人才团队所需的原料

### 五个妙招

检查你是否有以下这些：

1. 团队中必备的技术专家——你必须得推出核心产品和核心服务。

2. 团队内部对于未来挑战的目的和理解达成了共识——有才能的人对挑战总是跃跃欲试。对一个团队来说这点很重要，这样队伍中的每个人都能了解自己的贡献以及他人的贡献，也能有明确且一致的奋斗目标。

3. 互补而非雷同的性格特点。性格多样看上去似乎更难管理，但它造成的差异和冲突更能引导你的团队取得突破——只需一位出色的管理者。

4. 你手头的人才真正渴望帮助他人获得成功。他们不但要自己工作认真，也要关注团队的成果，不能只顾自己的业绩。

5. 你觉得可以信任的人——可以是你曾经的同事。

# CO-OPERATIVE OR CONTRIBUTORY TEAMS

There are different types of teams. Imagine two ends of a spectrum defined at the extremes as co-operative and contributory. What type of team do you lead? Are you focusing on the best things to drive the performance of your team?

| TEAM TYPE | CO-OPERATIVE | CONTRIBUTORY |
|---|---|---|
| Examples | Basketball, jazz band, football, customer service, cabin crew. | Cricket, sales teams, remote working, contact centre. |
| Performance Drivers | Ability to read the game, change positions, think and move for each other and spot the gaps in performance as they happen. | Focus on a common goal, desire to be the best you can, compete constructively with team colleagues, cheer others' success, deliver what you promise and recognise that every contribution matters. |

*Notes*

_____

_____

_____

_____

_____

人才搅拌器

## 合作式团队还是分担式团队

　　团队分为不同的类型。试想一条光谱的两头，一头叫做合作式，另一头叫做分担式。你领导的团队是哪种类型？你把关注重点放在提升团队绩效的关键点上了吗？

| 团队类型 | 合作式 | 分担式 |
|---|---|---|
| 例子 | 篮球、爵士乐队、足球、客户服务和空乘人员。 | 板球、销售团队、远程工作、联络中心。 |
| 提升绩效的驱动力 | 解读比赛、换位思考、为彼此着想、改变和察觉绩效差距的能力。 | 关注同一目标，希望能倾尽全力，与团队同事良性竞争，为他人的成功喝彩，信守自己的承诺，认识到每一份贡献都很重要。 |

## TALENT BLENDER

# CO-OPERATIVE OR CONTRIBUTORY TEAMS

| | | |
|---|---|---|
| **Team Values** | Your value to the team matters. One person can't win. | Personal targets based on talent and role. One person can make a big difference. |
| **Coach Focus** | Get people to play out of position so they understand different perspectives. | Get people to understand the value of own contribution towards a common goal. |
| | Encourage them to ask for help and look out for each other. | Encourage sharing of techniques and successes. |
| | Practise team communication and awareness. | Focus on planning ahead and accountability. |

*Notes*

_____

_____

_____

_____

_____

人才搅拌器

## 合作式团队还是分担式团队

| | | |
|---|---|---|
| **团队价值观** | 你的贡献对团队很重要,但光靠个人不会赢。 | 根据才能和职责设立个人目标。个人可以产生巨大影响。 |
| **教练重点** | 让员工转换角色做事,这样他们可以理解不同的观点。 | 让员工理解个人贡献对共同目标的意义。 |
| | 鼓励他们寻求相互帮助和关注彼此。 | 鼓励员工分享工作技巧和成功经验。 |
| | 进行团队交流,建立团队意识。 | 注意提前计划和责任意识。 |

## TALENT BLENDER

# CO-OPERATIVE OR CONTRIBUTORY TEAMS

| | | |
|---|---|---|
| **Talented People Must...** | Learn to play with each other, regardless of talent. | Recognise everyone matters. Compete constructively and help others learn. |
| **Analogy** | A beach ball – every side could be different depending on your perspective. | Cathedral – every brick matters. |

 *Notes*

_____

_____

_____

_____

_____

人才搅拌器

## 合作式团队还是分担式团队

|  | | |
|---|---|---|
| **人才<br>必须……** | 不论有无才华，都要学会合作。 | 认识到每个人都很重要。进行良性竞争，帮助他人学习。 |
| **类比** | 沙滩充气球——哪面都不一样，就看你从哪个角度看了。 | 大教堂——每块砖都很重要。 |

## TALENT BLENDER

# EQUAL TREATMENT FOR UNEQUAL TALENTS

The first lesson for any team leader is to realise that every team member should be treated as an individual and encouraged to make a personal contribution, to the best of their ability.

It is important, however, that you don't take this as a licence to focus solely on your favourite or best people. As a credible leader you must provide equal opportunity (which people may choose to take or not), and encourage others to be responsible for being the best that they can be. Some examples of things that should be provided equally:

✔ Time with you
✔ Access to suitable development opportunities
✔ Opportunity to have their say
✔ Reward for what they contribute

Examples of things that should not be equal:

✘ Actual level of responsibility they have (depends on competence)
✘ Accountability for results (depends on role and reward)
✘ Type of development activity (depends on individual needs)

*Notes*

_____

_____

_____

_____

_____

## 人才搅拌器

## 公平对待不同类型的人才

任何团队领导者要上的第一堂课是学会把每一位成员当作不同的个体来对待，鼓励他们尽自己的全力做出个人贡献。

不过，你不能以此为借口单单关注你最喜欢的员工或是最出色的员工，这点很重要。作为一位可靠的领导，你必须为所有员工提供平等的机会（他们可以选择接受或不接受），鼓励团队成员担起责任，尽自己最大的能力。举例来说，你应该平等提供的几样东西：

- ✓ 与你相处的时间
- ✓ 合适的发展机会
- ✓ 发言的机会
- ✓ 做出贡献的奖励

不该平等提供的几样东西：

- ✗ 员工实际的责任轻重（取决于能力）
- ✗ 对结果所负的责任（取决于职位和奖励）
- ✗ 培养活动的类型（取决于个人需求）

## TALENT BLENDER

# INTERDEPENDENCE

Small children are, initially, incredibly dependent. As they grow up they have periods of independence when they push away those they have previously relied on. Later that independence may be replaced with a more **interdependent** approach, when children accept and realise the power of working with others. The same can happen in a team, especially with talented people who are more capable of being independent of others.

| Dependent | Independent | Interdependent |
|---|---|---|
| You take care of me | I can do it | We can do it |
| You come through for me | I am responsible | We can co-operate |
| You didn't come through | I am self-reliant | We can combine our talents and abilities |
| I blame you for the results | I can choose | We can create something great together |
| I need others to get what I want | I can get what I want through my own efforts | My own efforts are best combined with the efforts of others to achieve success |

As managers we spend time encouraging people to make choices, be accountable, and take responsibility. The danger is that people will hear *'be independent'* rather than *'work together'*. Think about ways in which you can create interdependence.

*Notes*

_____

_____

_____

_____

_____

人才搅拌器

## 相互依赖

　　小孩生下来就特别有依赖心。在他们成长的过程中有几段独立期，这期间他们抛开了从前依赖的东西。而后，当他们承认并意识到与他人合作的力量后，这种独立性会被相互依赖性所取代。这个过程同样适用于一个团队，尤其是当团队成员都很出色、独立性很强的时候。

| 依赖 | 独立 | 相互依赖 |
|---|---|---|
| 你照顾我 | 我可以自己做 | 我们可以一起做 |
| 你帮我渡过难关 | 我来负责任 | 我们可以合作 |
| 你没帮我渡过难关 | 我靠我自己 | 我们可以结合彼此的才能 |
| 会这样都怪你 | 我自己做的决定 | 我们可以一起创造好东西 |
| 我需要其他人来帮我得到我想要的东西 | 我可以通过自己的努力得到我想要的东西 | 我自己的努力和别人的努力结合在一起取得的成效最好 |

　　作为管理者，我们需要花时间鼓励员工做决定、担责任、负责任。风险在于员工往往听到的是"自己来"而不是"一起做"。想些办法让员工彼此依赖。

# MANAGING PRIMA DONNAS

Talent is:

- A genius for making things happen...
- With a minimum fuss...
- Inspiring others to do the same

What do you do when you have a person with raw talent? A hotheaded, explosive character whose excellence demands a place in the team? A prima donna who will demand your time and could destroy the overall team? Every team can thrive on an injection of talent if the core is well balanced. We know that well respected, strong team members will usually have a positive influence on prima donnas, so you are not on your own. We also know that visible and agreed team values may make self-governance and discipline easier.

However, it's a straight cost benefit analysis, so get out a blank sheet of paper, draw a line down the middle and start listing the pro's and con's. See next page for examples.

*Notes*

_____

_____

_____

_____

_____

人才搅拌器

## 管理傲才

人才：

- 特别擅长落实任务……
- 遇事沉着冷静……
- 激励别人向他看齐

你怎么处理手头的璞玉？一个性急又冲动，可是才华横溢而必须给他个职位的员工？一个恃才傲物的人，既要花费你的时间又可能毁了整个队伍？一个团队只要核心成员职权平衡，加入新的人才也依然会茁壮成长。我们都知道，德高望重、实力强大的成员通常会对傲才产生积极的影响，所以你有帮手。我们也知道明确而一致的团队价值观会促进独立性和自律性。

不过，这只是个简单的得失分析，请拿出一张白纸，从中间竖着画一条线，开始列举利弊点。详例请见下页。

## TALENT BLENDER

# MANAGING PRIMA DONNAS

| FOR | AGAINST |
|---|---|
| ✔ Will make a significant difference to our result | ✘ Emotional outbursts will upset other team members |
| ✔ Will raise the standard for others | ✘ I will need to dedicate more of my time to managing the person and the fallout |
| ✔ Will add drive and energy that has been lacking recently | ✘ We may lose other team members |
| ✔ We have someone who could mentor the person | ✘ The team aren't cohesive enough to handle someone like this |

Your analysis may help you realise that sometimes prima donnas can just be too much of a risk, in which case manage without them, however talented they are!

For more ideas on how best to blend your talented people read the *Teambuilding Activities Pocketbook*.

*Notes*

---

## 人才搅拌器

### 管理傲才

| 同意 | 反对 |
|------|------|
| ✓ 会显著改善工作成果 | ✕ 情绪过激会干扰其他成员 |
| ✓ 会提升其他人的水平 | ✕ 我得花更多的时间来管这个人，收拾他搅起的波澜 |
| ✓ 会注入最近正缺少的动力和能量 | ✕ 我们可能会失去其他团队成员 |
| ✓ 我们有人能教导这个人 | ✕ 队伍凝聚力没强大到可以应付这样的人 |

　　你分析后可能会意识到某些情况下启用傲才的风险太大，那么还是别用了，不管这个人有多出色！

　　有关其他人才融合的好方法，可参阅《团队建设活动口袋书》。

## TALENT BLENDER

# A LONG-TERM APPROACH

*"'I did not set out to build a team: the task ahead was much bigger than that. What I really embarked on was the building of a system which would produce not one team but four or five, each occupying a rung on the ladder, the summit of which was the first XI."*

Consider the approach of Sir Matt Busby, the all-time great football manager, to developing his team.

- How do you view developing a team – a marathon or a sprint?

- How well are you using rising talent to provide healthy competition?

- When someone gets a promotion or leaves, what do you have in place to sustain the future success of the team?

## Notes

_____

_____

_____

_____

_____

# 人才搅拌器

## 长期策略

"我并不打算建一支球队：今后的任务比这个宏大得多。我真正从事的是一个体制的建立，建成后得到的可不是一支球队，而是四支甚至五支，每一支队伍占据一个梯级，最上面的那层就是先发的 11 人。"

借鉴一下历史上最伟大的足球教练马特·巴斯比爵士培养自己球队的方法。

• 你怎么看待团队建设——是马拉松还是冲刺跑？

• 利用不断成长的人才进行良性竞争，这点你做得怎么样？

• 如果某人升职或是离职了，你有什么措施来维持团队未来的成功？

## TALENT BLENDER

# A LONG-TERM APPROACH

Here are some ideas that any manager can adopt to shift to a longer-term, more sustainable approach to developing teams:

- Share the development projects and challenges around
- Rotate jobs even if that means a temporary drop in team performance
- Write things down – excellence is as much to do with great processes as it is the ability of a few great people
- Treat your core well, not just your talented people
- Initiate talent-spotting outside your team – think of it as an internal search. Talk to other managers and look for opportunities to move people around
- Spend some time on teambuilding and cohesion, including the teams and suppliers you work most closely with
- Pace yourself and make time for playing together
- If possible, be flexible about when and where your people work together

## Notes

_____

_____

_____

_____

_____

# 人才搅拌器

## 长期策略

　　管理人员培养团队时若想转而采取一种更为长期持久的策略，这里有些方法可以使用：

- 和身边的人分享人才培养项目及其困难

- 职位轮换，即便这么做会让团队绩效暂时下降

- 做记录——要做好一件事情，绝佳的流程和少数几位人才的能力一样重要

- 好好对待你的核心成员，而不单单是照顾有才华的员工

- 着手在你的团队之外搜寻人才——把它当做一种内部搜索。和其他的管理人员交流，找机会让人员流动起来

- 花一些精力建设团队，增强凝聚力，包括和其他与你工作联系密切的团队以及供应商

- 为自己定好节奏，抽时间聚会

- 如果可能的话，别太限制员工一起工作的时间和地点

# 人才指挥官

How can I create a flow of talented people?

**我怎样才能不断创造人才?**

## TALENT CONDUCTOR

# HEALTHY BELIEFS ABOUT TALENT

It is important to know how your senior managers collectively view talent management. Here are some unhealthy beliefs:

✗ *Life is about hard knocks so we should make it tough for our people*
✗ *Our HR department does a great job managing talent*
✗ *The ability to deliver is the only good indicator of potential, other than qualifications, obviously!*

Here are a few healthier ones:

✔ Every senior manager is accountable for spotting and developing talented people
✔ Developing a talent flow should be part of the business planning timetable
✔ Developing future senior managers needs real collaboration between all areas
✔ Talented people thrive in a performance culture
✔ Talented people learn by being stretched so use them to best effect
✔ Overall performance is a blend of the 'what' and 'how'; a shortfall in either must be dealt with quickly

Get views from your senior team and record them; then discuss the impact on the business.

*Notes*

人才指挥官

## 正确的人才观

　　了解高级管理人员对人才管理的整体看法非常重要。以下是一些不太高明的想法：

　　✕ 生活原本就充满打击，我们应该严格对待自己的员工
　　✕ 我们的人力资源部把人才管理得很好
　　✕ 撇开资历不谈，能否完成任务显然是员工潜力的唯一指标！

　　下面是一些比较高明的想法：

　　√ 每一位高级管理人员都有责任寻找和培养人才
　　√ 培养人才队伍应该被纳入业务计划日程表
　　√ 培养未来的高级管理人员需要各个部门切实的合作
　　√ 人才在绩效文化中不断成长
　　√ 人才在不断的伸展中学习，好好利用这点
　　√ 全局表现是"是什么"和"怎么做"的结合；哪一方面没到
　　　位都要尽快处理

　　询问你的高层团队的看法，记录下来，然后探讨它对业务的影响。

## TALENT CONDUCTOR

# DEFINING PERFORMANCE

Encourage your organisation to take a broad view of performance to include both what gets done (objectives) and how it gets done (behaviours). Once you have undertaken this you can discuss where your organisation draws the lines to define 'best', 'valued' and 'less effective'.

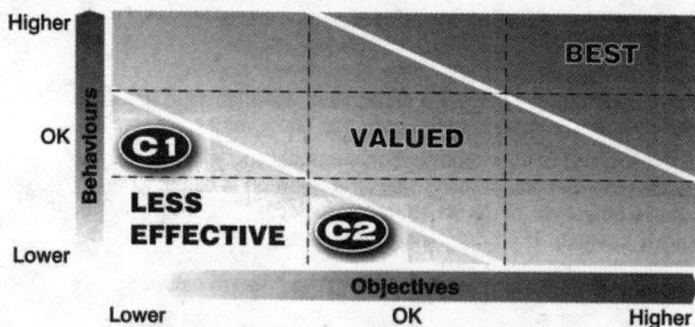

*Notes*

_____

_____

_____

_____

_____

# 人才指挥官

## 定义绩效

建议你任职的机构在绩效考核上考虑层面广一些，把做了什么（目标）和怎么做（行为）都包括进去。一旦你这么来做，就可以讨论你的机构确定"表现最佳"、"值得重视"和"效率低下"的界限在哪儿了。

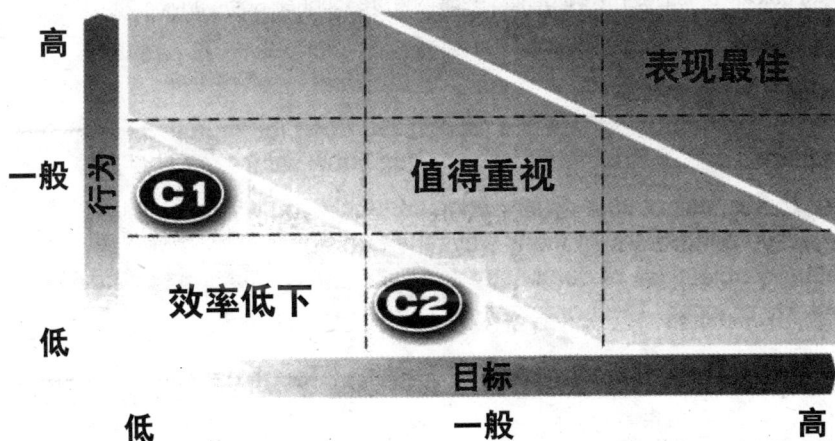

## TALENT CONDUCTOR

# DEFINING PERFORMANCE

**Best performers**
The very best contributors within the company. Consistently exceed and outpace changing expectations and are role models for our behaviours.

**Valued performers**
Strong contributors to business performance. Demonstrate our behaviours and keep pace with expectations.

**Less effective performers**
Least effective contributors. There is a recognised need for improvement in achieving objectives and/or demonstrating behaviours that show values are shared.

If you take the success of your organisation seriously you will act positively to deal with the less effective performers. In many ways the decision is easier with someone who doesn't achieve objectives or demonstrate the expected behaviours – they have to shape up very quickly or leave. The borderline decisions are tougher. Some advice:

**C1** Give them another chance in another role

**C2** Tough call, but you probably need to replace them

## Notes

_____

_____

_____

_____

_____

人才指挥官

## 定义绩效

### 最佳员工

公司中贡献最大的员工。不断超越预期，比预期进步得更快，是我们工作的榜样。

### 值得重视的员工

对公司业绩有较强的贡献，能起表率作用，紧跟预期。

### 效率低下的员工

工作效率最差的员工。不管是在完成目标还是在体现共同价值的行为方面都明显需要改善。

如果你重视自己任职机构的成功，你会积极采取行动应对低效率的员工。很多情况下决定比较好做，没能完成目标或表现上没达到预期水平的员工必须赶快进入状态，否则就得走人。针对边缘人物的决策就难一点了。给一些建议：

**C1** 在另一个职位上再给他们一次机会

**C2** 有些难办，不过恐怕你得换掉他们了

## TALENT CONDUCTOR

## TALENT PROFILER

It is important that the decisions you take about your talented people are well informed, eg investing in training, the nature and timing of their next move. What information do you need at your fingertips? What is the talent profile you need for each person in your team?

> *"Simplicity is the ultimate sophistication."*
> Leonardo da Vinci

The following four areas are a good place to start building a talent profile.

| | |
|---|---|
| **Track Record** | What they **can** do |
| **Potential Predictors** | What they **could** do |
| **Personal Aspirations** | What they **want** to do |
| **Readiness** | When they will be **ready** to do it |

Once you have a talent profile you can start to grapple with other questions such as:

- Who else needs to see the profile
- How you can keep the information current and accurate
- Who should own the profile
- How transparent the information should be

*Notes*

## 人才档案员

　　在作出有关人才的决策时，一定要了解他们的相关信息，这点很重要。比如培训上的投入、下次调职的理由和时机等。你需要对哪些信息了若指掌？你队伍中的每位成员需要怎样的人才档案？

> *"简约是极端的复杂。"*
> **——列奥纳多·达·芬奇**

　　以下四个领域是着手建立人才档案的好选择。

| | |
|---|---|
| **业绩记录** | 他们**能**做什么 |
| **潜力预测** | 他们**可能**做什么 |
| **个人志向** | 他们**想**做什么 |
| **准备就绪** | 他们何时**准备**好去做 |

　　一旦人才档案建立，你就可以开始处理其他的问题，比如：

- 谁还要看这份档案
- 你如何保证信息及时、准确
- 谁应该拥有这份档案
- 这些信息应该有多公开

## TALENT CONDUCTOR

## TALENT PROFILER

| TRACK RECORD | | POTENTIAL PREDICTORS | | PERSONAL ASPIRATIONS | | READINESS |
|---|---|---|---|---|---|---|
| What do we already know about someone that is relevant to profiling potential? | **+** | Predictors of whether someone has the potential to succeed in a bigger and/or more senior role | **+** | An indication of an individual's personal ambition and interest | **=** | An indication of the readiness of someone to make the next move and to what level |

The following pages will show how to build your own talent profile

*Notes*

_____

_____

_____

_____

_____

人才指挥官

## 人才档案员

| 业绩记录 | | 潜力预测 | | 个人志向 | | 准备就绪 |
|---|---|---|---|---|---|---|
| 对于要建档观察的对象我们已经掌握了哪些信息？ | ✚ | 预测某人是否能承担更大的责任或胜任更高的职位 | ✚ | 表明个人的志向和兴趣 | ＝ | 表明某人是否为进一步调职做好了准备，以及该调至哪个级别的职位 |

> 下面几页会向你展示如何建立自己的人才档案

**TALENT CONDUCTOR**

# TRACK RECORD

There are three distinct areas that come together to create a track record of performance.

**Achievement**    **What have they done?**
**Attitude**    **How did they bring it about?**
**Ability**    **What knowledge and skills did they display?**

The achievement of agreed objectives, the personal contribution someone makes, eg projects completed, usually provides a good assessment of **achievement**, often stated as a performance rating.

In a similar way, **attitude** is often assessed against a predetermined set of expected and observable competencies or behaviours.

**Ability** is the proven and relevant knowledge and skills developed from experience, eg effectively managing remote teams.

Every organisation will have its own ways of tracking achievement, attitude and ability. What information should you have at your fingertips about track record?

*Notes*

_____

_____

_____

_____

_____

人才指挥官

## 业绩记录

业绩记录由三种不同方面的内容共同组成。

**成就**　　他们完成了什么？
**态度**　　他们怎么做到的？
**能力**　　他们从中展现了哪些知识与技能？

共同目标的实现和个人做出的贡献（比如完成了的项目），一般可以用来正确地评估**成就**，且常常以绩效打分的方式进行。

同样，**态度**经常通过事先确定的一系列可预测、可观察的能力或行为来进行评测。

**能力**是从经验中得到并证实的相关知识和技能，比如有效地进行远距离团队管理。

每一个机构都有自己记录成就、态度和能力的方式。你应该了解哪些关于业绩记录的知识？

# TALENT CONDUCTOR

# INDICATORS OF POTENTIAL

A strong track record alone is not a great predictor of future success at a higher level. Often good people are promoted just one step too far and are set up for failure and frustration. It is possible with research, however, to identify which traits are reasonably good predictors of success within your organisation. The examples below are based on research within one organisation – what are your predictors?

| | Track Record | Indicators of Potential |
|---|---|---|
| Achievement | Achievement of performance objectives | ✔ Handles pressure effectively and makes the job look easy<br>✔ Challenges the boundaries of role. Keen to take on new, bigger challenges<br>✔ Orientated towards business results, not just focused on success of own area |
| Attitude | Demonstration of desirable behaviours | ✔ Confidence to take the lead<br>✔ Determined, resilient and prepared to be unpopular<br>✔ Natural enthusiasm and positive outlook<br>✔ Credible interpersonal skills with people at all levels in the company |
| Ability | Evidence of knowledge and skills | ✔ Understands and acts quickly and effectively in new/complex situations<br>✔ Receptive and open to new ideas and feedback and adapts how they work<br>✔ Exhibits technical and professional skills that are both broad and deep |

*Notes*

_____

_____

_____

_____

_____

人才指挥官

## 潜力预测指标

　　仅仅一份优秀的业绩记录并不能正确预判一位员工在更高职位上未来的成就。经常有优秀的员工被提拔到过高的职位，只能等着失败受挫。不过，我们可以通过研究确定在自己的机构中哪些特质代表一个人将来很可能会取得成功。以下这个例子是某一机构的研究结果——你的预测指标是什么？

| | 业绩记录 | 潜力预测指标 |
|---|---|---|
| 成就 | 完成绩效目标 | ✓有效处理压力，简化工作<br>✓对职权的界限提出质疑。渴望承受新的、更大的挑战<br>✓关注公司的业绩成果，不单单关注自己领域的成绩 |
| 态度 | 表现出公司期望的行为 | ✓有带头的自信<br>✓有决心，适应力强，做好了不受欢迎的准备<br>✓天生热情，态度积极<br>✓与公司各个级别的人员都能很好地交流 |
| 能力 | 知识和技能的证明 | ✓面对新的或复杂的情况，理解应对的速度快，效率高<br>✓容易接受新观念和反馈，对工作方式作出调整<br>✓展示出广泛渊博的专业和职业技能 |

## TALENT CONDUCTOR

# READINESS

Everyone contributes to success and is capable of more but only some have the potential to perform in a larger role. Honest, accurate assessment and feedback are at the heart of managing talent. In determining readiness you need to bring together an assessment of potential and the time required to achieve it. How do you want to describe and categorise potential? What language exists or would work in your organisation? The following example takes the position that everyone has at least some potential:

- **High potential** – very likely to compete successfully for, and succeed in, higher level roles within two years
- **Growth potential** – expect to be able to succeed in larger jobs at a similar level, with potential to move upwards in the longer term
- **Stretch potential** – likely to remain in position or move to a role with similar responsibilities; will develop expertise.

Don't forget about personal aspirations: it is essential for any talent manager to know what drives an individual. There is no science to this – simply ask them. The accuracy of the self-assessment is improved by the quality of feedback they have had and the openness of your relationship. **Without aspiration, potential is of little value.**

*Notes*

---

---

---

---

---

## 人才指挥官

### 准备就绪

　　每个人都可以为成功出一份力，而且能做到更多，但只有某些人有潜力承担更大的职责。人才管理的核心是忠实、准确的评估和反馈。在确定员工是否准备就绪这方面，你需要同时对员工潜力和胜任这项工作所需的时间进行分析。你想怎么描述、归类潜力？你的机构中用的是哪种风格的语言，又是哪种风格最有效果？以下的例子认为每个人都多少有点潜力：

　　**·潜力大**——两年内很有可能会在更高的职位竞争中胜出并取得成就

　　**·成长潜力**——可以在同级别职位中胜任更大的职责，长久来看有可能升职

　　**·伸展潜力**——很可能留在原职，或改任职责相似的职位；会发展专业能力

　　不要忘了个人志向：任何一位人才管理者都必须了解一个人的驱动力是什么。这没有什么技术含量——只要问问他们就好。对员工高质量的反馈以及你与他们之间的坦诚可以提高他们自我测评的准确性。**没有志向，潜力就没什么价值。**

# NINE BOX MODEL – AIRLINE STYLE

The nine box model is a talent management classic, first used in General Electric. Simply by combining an assessment of potential and performance you can better differentiate your talent strategies.

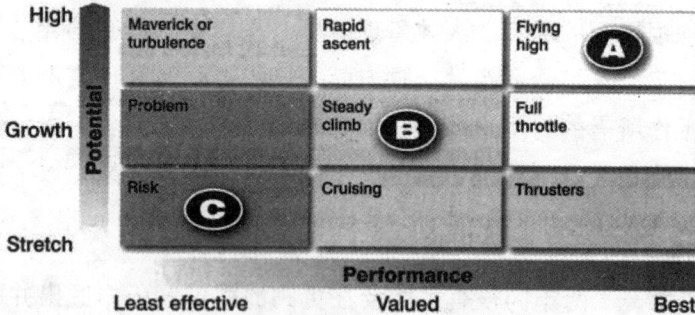

| Potential | Least effective | Valued | Best |
|---|---|---|---|
| **High** | Maverick or turbulence | Rapid ascent | Flying high **A** |
| **Growth** | Problem | Steady climb **B** | Full throttle |
| **Stretch** | Risk **C** | Cruising | Thrusters |

**Performance**

*Notes*

_____

_____

_____

_____

_____

人才指挥官

## 九宫格模型——航空公司风格

　　九宫格模型是人才管理的经典理论，最早用于通用电气。只要把潜力评估和员工表现相结合，你就可以更好地区分自己的人才战略。

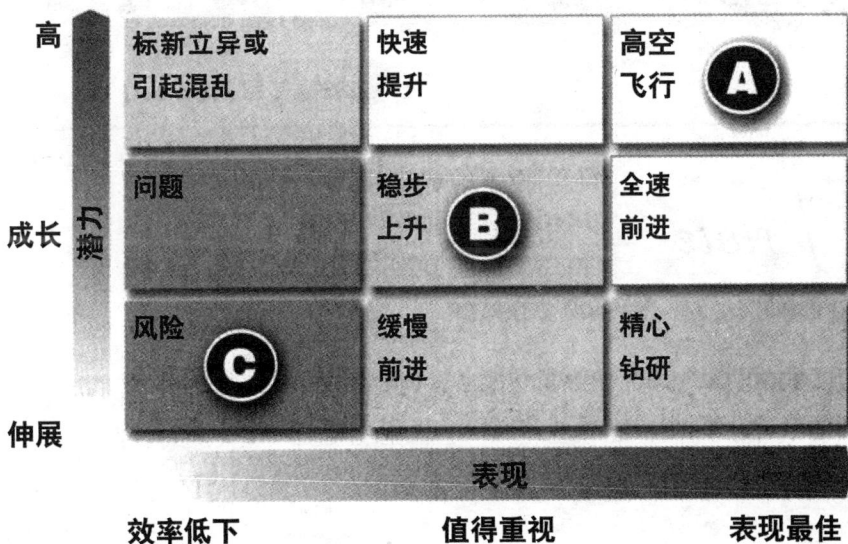

| 潜力 | 效率低下 | 值得重视 | 表现最佳 |
|---|---|---|---|
| **高** | 标新立异或引起混乱 | 快速提升 | 高空飞行 **A** |
| **成长** | 问题 | 稳步上升 **B** | 全速前进 |
| **伸展** | 风险 **C** | 缓慢前进 | 精心钻研 |

表现

## TALENT CONDUCTOR

# THE A, B, C's

The power of the nine box model comes when you are able to consistently apply the approach across the whole organisation – everyone understands the definitions and implications of the placement within the nine boxes. At its best senior managers will complete the exercise as part of the strategic timetable – determining the bench strength of the organisation, level by level.

The placement of people within the model should be subject to challenge and agreement from the wider leadership team. In many ways the discussion about talent and the transparency it creates is more powerful than the placement itself.

The nine box model must lead to decisions about talent.
For example:

**A** Retain at all costs, leaders to watch and stretch

**B** Keep if you can and develop

**C** Improve or lose

---

*Notes*

_____

_____

_____

_____

_____

人才指挥官

## A、B、C

如果你能持之以恒地将九宫格模型运用到整个机构，它的力量就会显现——人人都能理解九个格子布局的意思和内涵。最理想的状态下，高级管理人员会把这个练习提上战略日程表——以此确定机构的各级后备团队实力。

人员在这个模型中的位置应该服从大领导团队安排的任务和制定的共识。很多时候，有关人才的讨论及其透明度比人员在九宫格中的位置安排更有作用。

九宫格模型势必会引发人才方面的讨论。

比如：

**A** 不惜一切代价也要留下，保持关注，使其全力以赴，可作为领导培养

**B** 能留就留，进行培养

**C** 水平提高不了就辞掉

## TALENT CONDUCTOR

# PLACE YOUR BETS

What kind of talent do you have on your hands? Sometimes you don't have the luxury of promoting the perfect candidate. Where would you place your bet if the picture was less than perfect?

| Ability + Track record | only = | A high performer who is proven over time but may not have the aspiration, drive or organisational commitment to reach the next level. |
|---|---|---|
| Ability + Attitude | only = | A high performer who is currently performing well but not yet consistently proven over time. |
| Track record + Attitude | only = | A high performer who is already operating at the ideal level and may not have the ability to succeed in more senior roles. |

Ability and attitude would be a strong bet – with the individual having the opportunity to develop a track record. How often do we pick the track record as the best indicator of potential?

## Notes

_____

_____

_____

_____

_____

# 人才指挥官

## 下赌注

你手头有哪种类型的人才？有时情况没理想到可以提拔最佳人选。如果情况没那么完美，你会把赌注押在谁身上？

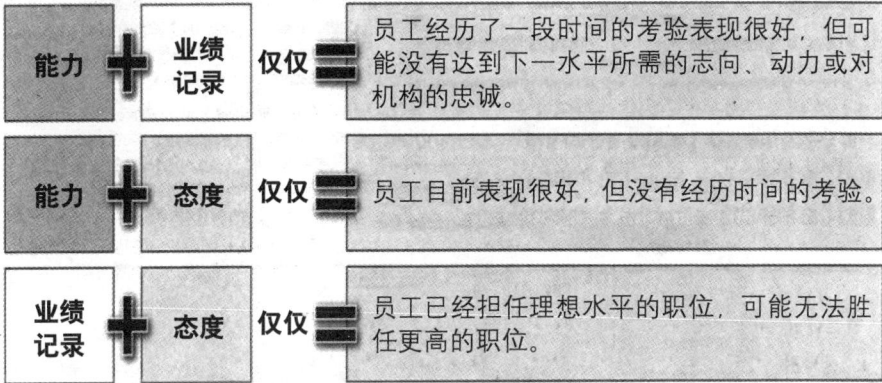

| 能力 + 业绩记录 仅仅 = | 员工经历了一段时间的考验表现很好，但可能没有达到下一水平所需的志向、动力或对机构的忠诚。 |
| 能力 + 态度 仅仅 = | 员工目前表现很好，但没有经历时间的考验。 |
| 业绩记录 + 态度 仅仅 = | 员工已经担任理想水平的职位，可能无法胜任更高的职位。 |

能力和态度是重要的赌注——前提是员工有建立业绩记录的机会。我们多常把业绩记录作为最重要的潜力指标？

# TALENT CONDUCTOR

## ASSESSMENT

Many talent management activities involve the need to confidently assess people's potential or performance. There are many ways to do this, and an equally diverse range of tools and techniques, ranging from manager assessment to psychologist designed assessment centres. How to assess is beyond the scope of this book, but here are some top tips to make assessment more readily accepted by those being assessed.

- Be clear how the assessment will be used, eg to decide development priorities vs selection for promotion
- Keep the assessment real – ground it in the context and pressures of the business
- Always provide quality feedback
- Build a robust personal development plan for all involved, not just those successful

- Celebrate the strengths identified
- Involve non-HR people in the assessment and invest in assessor training
- Keep it balanced – use 'track record' information as well as what you learn from the assessment process
- Consider the message you send to those who are not successful and who aren't selected for assessment – they'll know who they are

*Notes*

_____

_____

_____

_____

_____

人才指挥官

## 评估

　　很多人才管理活动包括对员工潜力或表现的明确评估。进行这种活动有许多方法，也同样有各种工具和技巧，从管理者测评到心理学家设计的评估中心，各种各样。评估的方法本书不予细谈，不过可以在这里提供一些小诀窍，让受评人更乐意接受评估。

· 讲明评估的作用，比如，是为了确定优先发展项目或为升职作筛选

· 保证评估的真实性——基于业务背景和压力

· 提供高质量的反馈

· 为所有参与人员制定稳健的发展计划，不单单只针对较为出色的员工

· 对发现的长处予以表扬

· 让人力资源部以外的员工参与评估，花功夫做测评员的培训

· 做好权衡——利用好"业绩记录"上的信息和你在评估过程中得到的信息

· 考虑评估活动对那些不够优秀、未入选评估的员工传递的信息——他们会知道自己的水平

## TALENT CONDUCTOR

# PEBBLES – POLISH OR PICK

When you look at a beach you see pebbles – piles of dull stones all looking much the same. You know that amongst them will be pebbles with amazing colours and fantastic shapes – you just need to polish them! Where do you start? Do you pick a few pebbles that look promising and give them a polish, accepting that you won't always make the right choice, or polish as many as you can straight away.

Your decision whether to 'pick and polish' or 'polish and pick' is an early one you need to make in any talent management approach. Do you invest your money in assessment of a select few or do you invest in broader development allowing the best to shine through?

If you are interested in the following, then pick before you polish:

- ✔ Confirming potential
- ✔ Targeting development investment
- ✔ Guiding placement and selection decisions

If you are interested in the following, then polish before you pick:

- ✔ Building capability in the organisation
- ✔ Getting people ready for a job challenge
- ✔ Developing competencies
- ✔ Identifying personality traits

*Notes*

---

---

---

---

---

人才指挥官

## 鹅卵石——打磨还是筛选

　　环顾海滩，你会看见很多鹅卵石——一堆堆乏味的石头，看上去都差不多。你知道其中有色彩夺目、形状奇特的鹅卵石——你只需打磨它们！从哪儿开始呢？你会选几个看上去不错的先打磨（虽然你知道自己的决定不一定正确），还是马上动手，能打磨几个就打磨几个？

　　不论你采取哪种人才管理方法，你需要尽早决定是"先筛选再打磨"还是"先打磨再筛选"。你想把钱花在评估自己选出来的几个人身上还是多培养一些，让最优秀的人自己闪光？

如果你对以下几项感兴趣，那就先筛选再打磨：

✓确认潜力
✓瞄准投资培养的对象
✓对人员安置和筛选决策做指导

如果你对以下几项感兴趣，那就先打磨再筛选：

✓在组织内构建能力
✓让员工为工作中的挑战做好准备
✓培养能力
✓鉴别性格特点

## TALENT CONDUCTOR

# LETTING YOUR TALENT KNOW

Do you let your talented people know they are earmarked as high potential? Do they already know? Who else needs to know and will others find out? How transparent do you make your decisions? Letting people know has the following advantages and disadvantages:

**Advantages**
- ✔ Motivating for talent
- ✔ Public recognition for people
- ✔ Focuses the minds of nominating managers
- ✔ Something to work towards
- ✔ Gives out message that company values talent – aids recruitment

**Disadvantages**
- ✘ Demotivating for others; those not picked out feel undervalued
- ✘ Weak managers may avoid tough decisions
- ✘ Creates higher expectations in those selected
- ✘ Your talent may develop prima donna tendencies
- ✘ Will expose frailties in basis of selection, eg performance

The decision will be influenced by what is on offer as a result of selection, eg: accelerated development, reward, number of people involved in the assessment, openness of company culture and expectation of employees.

*Notes*

## 人才指挥官

## 让人才知道你的期望

你会让你的人才知道他们被寄予厚望吗？他们是不是已经知道了？还有谁需要知道，别人会不会发现？你决策的透明度如何？让员工知道你的期望有如下优点和缺点：

**优点**

✓ 鼓舞人才

✓ 让员工得到普遍认可

✓ 集中人事经理的注意力

✓ 是一种工作动力

✓ 传递出公司重视人才的信息——对招聘有利

**缺点**

× 挫败其他员工的积极性；没被选中的人觉得自己被低估了

× 能力差的管理者可能会回避艰难的选择

× 让被选中的人产生过高的期待

× 你的人才可能会有傲才倾向

× 会暴露筛选基准的脆弱，比如绩效

决定怎么做需要考虑筛选后待遇的变化，比如培养速度的提升、奖金、参与评估的人数、企业文化的公开度以及员工的期待等。

**TALENT CONDUCTOR**

# SUPPORT KEY TRANSITIONS

Promotions rarely lead to a smooth progression. The step change between some roles can make it difficult to adapt quickly. This is particularly the case if the change is one of the key transitions, eg from managing self to managing people or from managing people to managing managers.

As mentioned on page 118, **performance in one role is not always a good predictor of performance in another**. It is these transitions that demand a fundamental change in what you value, your skills and perspective.

When developing talented people you must be aware of the challenges facing the individual. Looking at the example of someone making the transition from managing self to managing others you can ask:

1. Which values will drive success in the new role?
   Eg: *Making time for others*

2. What are the key new skills in the role?
   Eg: *Providing constructive feedback*

3. What perspective will be most valuable in the future?
   Eg: *Beyond the next 12 months*

*Adapted from: The Leadership Pipeline*

*Notes*

## 人才指挥官

### 支持关键转变

升职的过程很少一帆风顺。不同职位间步调的改变可能不容易很快适应。特别是关键职位变动的时候，比如，从自我管理到管理他人，或者从管理普通员工到管理经理。

如119页所言，**员工在一个职位上的表现并不一定能反映他在另一职位上的表现**。正是这种转变要求你工作的重心、你的技巧和视角都有本质的改变。

培养人才时，你必须认识到员工所面临的挑战。看看这个例子，某人从普通员工转为管理人员，你可以询问：

1. 要在新职位上取得成功需要哪种观念？
   例：为别人付出时间。

2. 这个职位上关键的新技能是什么？
   例：提供建设性的反馈。

3. 未来哪种看待问题的视角最重要？
   例：考虑未来12个月之后的事情。

*改编自《领导补给线》*

## TALENT CONDUCTOR

# SUCCESSION MANAGEMENT

Many companies like to put in place a succession plan – an elegant map of the organisation showing named successors and *just in case* people, with every risk identified and contingency plans in place. Is this a valuable use of time or a source of false confidence based on what appears to be a complete picture?

Organisations need to be able to respond rapidly to change and can no longer rely on the most talented people waiting patiently for the next step. Even the best laid plans can unravel over a relatively short period of time as roles and people change.

An alternative is to take a risk management approach to succession:

- Agree the roles which are key to future business success
- Determine the *what if* scenarios for each key role
- List the roles appearing to lack strength in depth and put in place a *talent flow* towards them
- Provide broad development opportunities based on an individual's aspirations
- Select the best available person when a vacancy does arise

*Notes*

人才指挥官

## 继任管理

　　许多公司喜欢制订继任者计划——一张漂亮的路线图上标着继任者的名字和以防万一的人选，每一种风险都考虑到了，应急计划也做好了。这么做是高效率地利用时间，还是一种盲目的自信，以为一切都已尽在掌握？

　　每个机构都要有迅速应对变化的能力，不能一直依赖最出色的人才，耐心等待下一步行动。即便是最精心的计划，也很快会在职位和人员的变动中分崩离析。

　　另一种安排继任者的方法是进行风险管理：

- 确定对未来业务成功至关重要的职位
- 为每一关键职位做好假设情境分析方案
- 列出看上去比较薄弱的几个职位，为它们准备好人才流
- 根据个人志向提供更广阔的发展机会
- 真的出现空缺时，任命你手头最合适的人选

## TALENT CONDUCTOR

# TALENT FORUM

Senior managers clearly have the accountability for talent management in any organisation. What forum do you have in place for the necessary conversations to take place and how often should the forum be convened? Consider the potential agenda items below and decide on the focus of your talent forum:

- Review the impact of your business strategy and key projects on the talent you need
- Review company culture eg employee opinion survey
- Challenge and benchmark the profile of performance ratings
- Assess the bench strength for senior and key roles
- Create space for development eg secondments, projects, rotation
- Make reward, bonus and recognition programme decisions
- Review key measures eg diversity, internal promotions and moves
- Agree the focus for 'development agenda' and resources for next period
- Develop a 'talent to watch' list and agree who will stay close to these people
- Hold the next level down accountable for shifting the 'C' list performers quickly

*Notes*

人才指挥官

# 人才讨论会

　　任何机构中的高级管理人员显然都负有人才管理的责任。为了员工间必要的交流，你安排了什么讨论会，多久召开一次？考虑以下组建讨论会的事项，确定你的人才讨论会关注的重点：

- 回顾你的业务战略和重点项目对你需要的人才产生的影响
- 总结公司文化，比如员工意向调查
- 对绩效考核提出质疑，并与其他同类型的公司作比较
- 评估高级职位和关键职位的后备实力
- 创造发展空间，例如外调、项目和人员轮岗
- 确定奖金、分红和奖励措施
- 复查关键的衡量标准，例如多样性、内部升职和调动
- 确定"发展计划"的重点，以及下一阶段的资源
- 列出"待观察人才"，确定谁来密切关注这些人
- 缩减专用于迅速替换"C"级绩效员工的后备级人员

## TALENT CONDUCTOR

## EMBEDDING TALENT MANAGEMENT INTO BUSINESS PLANNING

Just how important is talent management in your organisation? A good test is the extent to which the practices associated with it have been embedded into the business planning process. Follow the steps below for a good way to do this.

1. **List all the business activities that exist in your organisation, eg:**
   **Strategy** – development, communication and review
   **Operational** – planning, cascading, budgeting and forecasting
   **Communications** – executive level, operating reviews and conferences
   **Performance** – setting and reviewing performance objectives, 360 feedback and development planning
   **People** – employee survey and action planning, reward and recognition activities

2. **Draw a 12 month timeline and transfer each business activity to the appropriate part of the timeline**

*Notes*

---

---

---

---

人才指挥官

## 把人才管理纳入业务规划

在你任职的机构中人才管理究竟有多重要？最好的检测方法是看与此相关的措施有多少被纳入了业务规划之中。按以下步骤做就好。

**1. 列出你任职的机构中所有的业务活动，例如：**

**战略**——发展、交流和回顾
**运营**——计划、逐级下传、制定预算和预测
**沟通**——管理级别上、运营评估和会议
**绩效**——制定、回顾绩效目标，360度反馈和发展计划
**人员**——员工调查、业务计划、奖励及认可措施

**2. 制定 12 个月的时间表，把每一业务活动列入表中合适的位置**

## TALENT CONDUCTOR

## EMBEDDING TALENT MANAGEMENT INTO BUSINESS PLANNING

3. **Identify the dependencies between each activity**
   eg strategy development before operational planning

4. **Identify bottlenecks and opportunities to better align talent activities**
   eg employee survey results before operational planning, 360 feedback before strategic talent review

Share your map with others and agree on the best possible fit.

*Notes*

_____

_____

_____

_____

人才指挥官

## 把人才管理纳入业务规划

### 3. 明确每一活动之间的相互关系

例如，先确定战略再制定营运计划

### 4. 发现瓶颈和机遇，完善人才管理活动的流程

例如，等员工调查结果出来后再制定营运计划，先进行 360 度反馈再做战略人才评估

和别人探讨你的路线图，找出最合适的人选。

## TALENT CONDUCTOR

# FIVE DEVELOPMENT EXPERIENCES

According to Helen Handfield-Jones, *How Executives Grow*, the following five experiences provide the stretch to accelerate the development of leadership talent.

1. A new job with greater scope
2. Turning a business around
3. Starting a business
4. Managing a large project
5. Working abroad

> *"I hear and I forget, I see and I remember, I do and I understand"*
> Confucius

All talented people thrive on experiences which provide:

- Early leadership roles and significant responsibilities
- Increased pressure under which to try out skills
- Visual accountability for fix-it situations and results
- An opportunity to build and lead a team in tough situations
- Strong coaching and speedy feedback
- Cross functional and cross cultural experiences so you can learn from differences
- Encouragement to take risks with a soft(er) landing to help learning

## Notes

_____

_____

_____

_____

_____

## 人才指挥官

## 五种工作经历

海伦·汉德菲尔德－琼斯的《管理人员如何成长》一书中提到，以下五种经历可以加快领导才能的培养。

1. 职权更广的新职位
2. 扭转业务状况
3. 创业
4. 管理一个大项目
5. 海外任职

> "不闻不若闻之，闻之不若见之，见之不若知之，知之不若行之。"
> ——**孔子**

具有这些经历的人才发展势头良好：

- 很早就担任管理职位，有强烈的责任心
- 加压之下尝试培养新的能力
- 愿意收拾烂摊子，为后果承担责任
- 有机会在艰难的形势下组队领队
- 良好的教练，迅速的反馈
- 有跨职位跨文化的工作经历，可以从差异中学习
- 有备无患时，为了获取经验被鼓励冒险

**TALENT CONDUCTOR**

# TALENT SCORECARD

How do you measure the success of your talent management activities?

- % of your people who, if they applied today, would be picked
- Number of long-term vacancies
- Average time taken to fill vacancies
- Employee retention rates for key roles, performance levels and departments
- Balance between internal and external appointments
- Spend on contingent workers and consultants
- Quality perception of hiring managers
- Stakeholder satisfaction
- Quality of recruits, eg average time taken to reach competence
- Employee engagement index
- Shift in 360 degree or other feedback scores
- % people classified as A, B and C list
- % key roles with more than one potential internal replacement
- % people with a personal development plan
- Diversity and inclusion rates

*Notes*

# 人才指挥官

## 人才计分卡

你怎么衡量自己安排的人才管理活动是成功还是失败？

- 你手下的员工如果现在申请的话百分之多少会被选中
- 长期空缺的职位有多少
- 填补空职花费的平均时间
- 关键职位、各等级的职位以及各部门能留住的员工比例
- 内部任命和外部任命的平衡
- 在临时员工和顾问上的花费
- 招聘经理对员工素质的理解
- 利益相关者的满意程度
- 所招聘员工的素质，例如，胜任职位所需的平均时间
- 员工参与指数
- 360 度绩效考核分数的变化，或其他反馈分数的变化
- A、B、C 类员工所占的比例
- 关键职位有不止一位内部后备人员的百分比
- 有个人发展计划的员工的百分比
- 多样性、包容度

# 人才吸铁石

What will attract talented people and keep them for longer?

靠什么能吸引人才，让他们为我效力更久？

## TALENT MAGNET

# ATTRACT OR REPEL?

The big question is, *'why would talented people want to join your organisation?'*

How your organisation is seen in the outside world – your reputation – is something that will either act as a positive force to attract great employees or will repel the best from joining you. Answer these questions to develop an image of your reputation.

1. At your worst, how would your organisation or team be described?
2. When you shine, how would your organisation or team be described?
3. What does your organisation or team represent?
4. What makes your organisation or team stand out from your competitors?
5. What is the public image of your leadership team?

What conclusions can you draw from your answers? Are you describing an attractive employer, a company or team people would want to be associated with? What score out of 10 would you realistically give yourself? (0 = stinker, 10 = attractive). The lower your score the more likely you are to have to buy or grow your own talent. To reduce this likelihood (and expense) you may decide you need to actively manage your reputation.

*Notes*

_____

_____

_____

_____

_____

## 人才吸铁石

## 吸引还是排斥?

关键问题在于,"为什么人才想加入你的机构?"

外人对你的机构怎么看——你的名声——不是吸引出色员工的正向力,就是令优秀人才对你避之不及的反向力。回答以下问题,勾画出一幅你的名声图景。

1. 你做得最糟糕时,你的机构或团队会被说成什么样?
2. 如果你干得好,你的机构或团队会被说成什么样?
3. 你的机构或团队的特点是什么?
4. 你的机构或团队从竞争对手中脱颖而出靠的是什么?
5. 你的领导班子在大家心目中的形象如何?

你从自己的答案中得出的结论是什么?你口中所说的是一个让人趋之若鹜、有吸引力的雇主、公司或者团队吗?满分10分的话,你会给自己打几分? (0= 无人问津,10= 极有吸引力。)你的分数越低,就越有可能需要花钱买人才或是培养自己的人才。为了降低这种可能(也是花费),你可能要积极采取行动,管理自己的名声。

## TALENT MAGNET

# STICKY RECRUITMENT: TOP TIPS

The recruitment process is important, not just in making the best selection but also in bonding talent to the company. Recruiting should be *sticky* and the following will help you keep your best people even before you start.

- Involve your team in the process – talented people want to know who will help them realise their potential
- Provide an honest preview of the job – the talented thrive on a challenge or a fix-it situation
- Set the bar high – profile the company's successes and strengths so that talented people can see what they will learn; don't be modest!
- Explore and share values and motives – your company's, your own and the individual's. Overlap = stickiness
- Know your company's talent predictors – what your best people have got in common – and look for evidence in the interview
- Treat people well at recruitment – candidates are looking for clues about you and your organisation. Actively manage expectations and show as realistic a picture as possible. Talented people like to see a challenge

*Notes*

_____

_____

_____

_____

_____

人才吸铁石

## 有吸引力的招聘：重要窍门

　　招聘过程的重要性不仅在于作出最好的选择，还在于让人才和公司建立感情。招聘工作应该有吸引力，以下几个窍门让你尚未开始招聘，便留住了最优秀的人才。

　　·让你的团队成员加入招聘工作——人才想要知道帮助自己发挥潜力的人是谁

　　·对工作预先进行真实的介绍——人才是迎难而上、越挫越勇的

　　·设立高标准——简单介绍公司取得的成就和优势，让人才知道自己将会学到什么，别谦虚！

　　·探讨、分享价值观和动力——你公司的，你自己的，以及应聘者的。重叠＝粘性

　　·了解你公司人才的风向标——最出色的人才拥有的共通点——在面试中搜寻这一迹象

　　·招聘时好好对待应聘者——求职者正在寻找你和你们机构的蛛丝马迹。有效地控制期望值，情况描述得越真实越好。人才喜欢接受挑战

**TALENT MAGNET**

# GOOD RECRUITMENT PRACTICES

Man of the Match or Mates of Mine? Who gets the promotion and how the decision is made can make or break confidence in how your organisation manages talent. While a hiring manager must feel comfortable with whoever they appoint and may have invested in the development of some candidates, the final decision should always be the best affordable person. The following recruitment principles will encourage the best use of your talented people:

- Explore alternatives to permanent replacement to broaden their accountabilities
- Search the talent pool – based on specific aspirations and track record to identify 'hidden' talent outside your own team – to consider alongside talent within your area
- Advertise all new and replacement roles internally and externally
- Talk to your talent champions (see page 66)
- Consider evidence of personal development a positive indicator for selection and be prepared to take a *nearly ready* internal candidate and help them develop
- Ensure rigorous assessment of track record and potential at recruitment stage;

## Notes

_____

_____

_____

_____

_____

# 人才吸铁石

## 做好招聘工作

　　是对手还是队友？谁升职、如何决定的，是使应聘者信不信任你们机构人才管理方式的关键。虽然招聘经理对自己任命的人选一定是满意的，也可能对某几位候选人的培养花了心思，但最终选择的必须是最实惠的人员。以下这些招聘原则会让你最高效地使用人才：

　　• 探讨寻找某一职位的备用人才，扩大他们的职权

　　• 搜寻人才库——在你的团队之外，根据特定需要和业绩记录找出"隐藏的"人才——在人才库中搜寻

　　• 在团队内外宣传所有新职位或需要替换的职位

　　• 和你的人才的佼佼者谈谈（见 67 页）

　　• 把个人发展作为人才筛选的一项正面指标来考虑，准备好任用快要准备就绪的内部候选人，并帮助他们成长

　　• 保证对招聘阶段人员的业绩记录和潜力状态都做了认真评估；每一项都做到位

# TALENT MAGNET

## LOVE TO WORK

We would all prefer a happy workplace but in itself it is not enough. Those happy people may not be the ones who really respond under pressure, willingly share ideas and challenge how you operate; the people you can trust in tough times. Get beyond happy and into **engaged**, spread a little love – that's what drives performance.

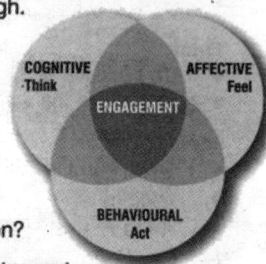

1. What do your best people **think** about your organisation?
2. How do your best people **feel** about your organisation?
3. What are your best people **willing to do** for your organisation?

In the diagram, the Cognitive or Think component relates to employees' logical evaluation of a company's goals and values. The Affective or Feel component taps into whether employees have a sense of belonging and pride. Finally, the Behavioural or Act dimension captures the outcomes that employers desire, eg retention and willingness to go the extra distance when necessary. Engagement itself is actually a measure of the combination of these three components.

*Notes*

_____

_____

_____

_____

_____

# 人才吸铁石

## 热爱工作

　　我们都希望办公室充满快乐，但单是快乐本身并不足够。快乐的员工可能在压力之下缺乏行动，不愿分享自己的想法，或是对你的运营方式从来没有疑义；不是你在艰难时刻可以信任的人。所以要超越快乐，做到**参与其中**，散播一点热爱——这才是提升业绩的动力。

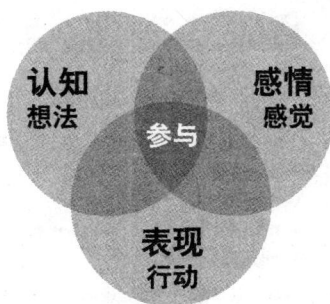

1. 你手头最优秀的人才如何**看待**你的机构？
2. 你手头最优秀的人才对你的机构**感觉**如何？
3. 你手头最优秀的人才**愿意**为你的机构做些什么？

　　图表中，认知或想法的部分是关于员工对公司目标和价值观的逻辑评估。感情或感觉的部分研究的是员工是否有归属感和自豪感。最后，表现或行动部分确定的是雇主期待的结果，比如，留住人才和在必要情况下敢于突破。参与本身其实考量的是这三个部分结合的效果。

**TALENT MAGNET**

# LOVE TO WORK

Some good questions to ask yourself or your people.

**Think**
- Do I believe in the vision and strategic ambitions of our organisation?
- Do I share the values for which our organisation stands?

**Feel**
- Am I proud to be part of this organisation?
- Would I recommend this organisation as a good employer?

**Act**
- Would it take much for me to look for another job elsewhere?
- Am I willing to put in extra effort for the organisation when it really matters?

You can ask these questions individually in focus groups, or ideally as part of a more complete employee opinion survey.

*Thanks to ISR. To find out more visit www.isrinsight.com*

*Notes*

---

# 人才吸铁石

## 热爱工作

下面这些问题可以拿来问问你自己和你的员工。

### 想法
- 我相信我们机构的愿景和战略雄心吗？
- 我认可我们机构的价值观吗？

### 感觉
- 我身为这个机构的一员感到骄傲吗？
- 我会向别人推荐这个机构，说它是个好雇主吗？

### 行动
- 我再另找一份工作难不难？
- 必要情况下，我愿意为这个机构付出更多心力吗？

你可以在讨论小组中一对一地问这些问题，或者最好把它纳入一个更为完善的员工意向调查表中。

感谢 ISR。想了解更多，请访问 www.isrinsight.com

## TALENT MAGNET

# WHAT MAKES TALENTED PEOPLE (S)TICK?

Talented people are naturally engaged and committed to success. When that loyalty fades and your best people leave or switch teams it doesn't mean their talent has faded. Managers with low magnetism will blame higher salaries or the predictable need for career progression.

The real reasons are more likely to be:

- Not getting the challenge that they crave
- Not being supported to achieve personal ambitions
- Not sharing the values of the company or the manager
- Not being cared for as an individual

Identify your best people and ask yourself:

- What challenges does this person have now?
- What challenges can I provide in the future?
- How can I explain the challenges in a compelling way?
- How can I prepare this person for the challenge and support them to achieve it?

Talented people expect recognition and reward for what they do. It is a good idea to differentiate the reward and recognition that someone can receive when they deliver results. In particular, try to balance the attention you pay to results and to the methods used to achieve them.

*Notes*

_____

_____

_____

_____

_____

## 人才吸铁石

## 留住人才需要什么?

　　人才天生就热衷于取得成功，也愿意为此付出。当这种忠诚度减退时，当你最好的员工离职或是转到其他团队时，并不代表他们的天赋消退了。吸引力弱的管理人员会把责任推到高薪或是可预计到的职业发展需求上。

真正的原因更可能是：

- 未能得到他们渴望的挑战
- 追求个人志向时没得到支持
- 与公司或经理的价值观不一致
- 作为个体没有受到照顾

找出你最优秀的员工，然后问自己：

- 目前这个人有哪些挑战?
- 未来我能提供哪些挑战?
- 我要怎么绘声绘色地描述这些挑战?
- 我怎么让这个人为挑战做好准备，并帮助他战胜挑战?

　　人才期待自己的工作得到认可和奖励。在他们完成工作后，最好根据情况区分开不同员工受到的奖励。特别是要试着平衡你对成果和取得成果的方法的关注度。

TALENT MAGNET

# EXCITING JOBS

**Talk to your best people to find out what makes them buzz.**
**How does your list compare?**

- The opportunity to 'move' when the personal challenge reduces
- Plenty of freedom, autonomy and responsibility
- Open doors that lead to talented and competent (role model) leaders
- Stimulating colleagues
- The space to try things, build on ideas and find solutions
- Someone who will show an interest in them and how they are doing
- A personal stretch but not defeat
- A steady flow of new ideas and projects
- Being able to make a direct and significant contribution to the business
- A fair wage **and** the tools to do the job

Your job as a talent manager is to listen carefully and spot the opportunities to create more buzz. What would make *your* workplace even more stimulating and motivating?

*Notes*

_____

_____

_____

_____

_____

人才吸铁石

## 令人振奋的工作

**和你最出色的员工交流，找出他们的兴奋点。
你的清单独特在哪儿?**

- 个人挑战减退时"离开"的机会
- 充分的自由、自主和足够大的职责
- 为员工成为有才华有能力（模范）的领导人才打开大门
- 使人振奋同事
- 作出尝试，构建想法，寻找解决办法的空间
- 有人对他们以及他们的表现感兴趣
- 对个人能力的伸展，但不是挫败
- 定期有新想法和新项目
- 能为业务作出直接且重要的贡献
- 公道的薪水**以及**工作所需使用的工具

　　作为人才管理者，你的工作是认真聆听他们的想法，抓住机会创造更多的兴奋点。能让你的办公室更令人振奋、更鼓舞人心的是什么?

## TALENT MAGNET

# HOW ATTRACTIVE IS YOUR TALENT CULTURE?

The following are questions talented people regularly ask themselves. How would your best people answer the questions?

| | YES | NO |
|---|---|---|
| 1. Can I learn from my manager? | ○ | ○ |
| 2. Do I know what is next for me? | ○ | ○ |
| 3. Can this organisation provide a fresh challenge and stretch? | ○ | ○ |
| 4. Can this organisation provide progression? | ○ | ○ |
| 5. Is there a problem that needs solving? | ○ | ○ |
| 6. Is this undertaking worthwhile? | ○ | ○ |
| 7. Do I feel comfortable with the values of this organisation? | ○ | ○ |
| 8. Do I get recognition for my efforts? | ○ | ○ |
| 9. Am I adding value here? | ○ | ○ |
| 10. Do I respect and value the people I am working with? | ○ | ○ |
| 11. Do I have the freedom to get on with my job? | ○ | ○ |
| 12. Can I be flexible in how, when and where I work? | ○ | ○ |

*Notes*

人才吸铁石

## 你们的人才文化有多吸引人？

人才经常会问自己以下问题。你最出色的员工会怎么回答？

| | 是 | 否 |
|---|---|---|
| 1. 我可以从经理身上学到东西吗？ | ○ | ○ |
| 2. 我知道自己下一步要做什么吗？ | ○ | ○ |
| 3. 这个机构可以为我提供新鲜的挑战和能力拓展吗？ | ○ | ○ |
| 4. 这个机构可以为我提供进步空间吗？ | ○ | ○ |
| 5. 有需要解决的问题吗？ | ○ | ○ |
| 6. 这份工作有价值吗？ | ○ | ○ |
| 7. 我认可这个机构的价值观吗？ | ○ | ○ |
| 8. 我付出的努力得到认可了吗？ | ○ | ○ |
| 9. 我为这里增值了吗？ | ○ | ○ |
| 10. 我尊重、珍视与我一起工作的人吗？ | ○ | ○ |
| 11. 我有开展工作的自由吗？ | ○ | ○ |
| 12. 我工作的方式、时间和地点有弹性吗？ | ○ | ○ |

## TALENT MAGNET

# HOW ATTRACTIVE IS YOUR TALENT CULTURE?

| | YES | NO |
|---|---|---|
| 13. Do I have the freedom to experiment, make mistakes and learn? | ◯ | ◯ |
| 14. Do I receive regular, honest, and candid feedback? | ◯ | ◯ |
| 15. Do I feel good about myself and what I am doing? | ◯ | ◯ |
| 16. Am I enjoying this? | ◯ | ◯ |
| 17. Am I stimulated? | ◯ | ◯ |

How would your best people score your team?

0 to 5     They have probably dusted off the CV and you'll need to act quickly and honestly to persuade them to stick around.

6 to 12     Good job! You are likely to be attractive to talented people but complacency may be your undoing. Check out the areas you didn't score as Yes and find a way to shift your score upwards.

13 to 17     Such is your attractiveness you must be turning great people away. Congratulations, please share your expertise with others in your organisation.

*Notes*

## 人才吸铁石

### 你们的人才文化有多吸引人?

| | 是 | 否 |
|---|---|---|
| 13. 我有尝试、犯错和学习的自由吗? | ◯ | ◯ |
| 14. 我能收到真实可靠的定期反馈吗? | ◯ | ◯ |
| 15. 我对自己和现在所做的工作满意吗? | ◯ | ◯ |
| 16. 我乐在其中吗? | ◯ | ◯ |
| 17. 我受到激励了吗? | ◯ | ◯ |

你最优秀的人才会给你的团队打多少分?

0-5 分　　他们恐怕又把简历拿出来了,你得尽快采取切实的行动,劝说他们留下。

6-12 分　　干得好!你对人才有一定的吸引力,不过自满可能是你的软肋。审视一下答案为否的地方,想办法提高得分。

13-17 分　　你对人才的吸引力极强,恐怕一直忙着拒绝找上门来的人才吧。恭喜你,请你与机构中的其他人分享自己的专长。

## TALENT MAGNET

## FINAL THOUGHTS

So what is the future for talent? There is much that will influence how we get the best from our talented people. For example, technology and legislation will drive an agenda of flexible working practices. Global and environmental challenges will influence the perspective of people away from traditional ways of working.

My final thoughts have to be about being flexible and responsive when defining how you will work with your talented people. Be flexible about how you expect them to work, when and where you want them to work and even the work you ask them to do.

Remember:
- Variety is naturally refreshing and change itself broadens perspective as you learn from differences
- Flexibility encourages people to explore more and see things afresh
- Relaxation is one of the best ways to stimulate creativity (just think about how your mind wanders in the shower or when you're exercising)

I hope this book has stimulated some ideas and inspired you to do things differently.

Good luck!

 *Notes*

_____

_____

_____

_____

_____

# 人才吸铁石

## 结语

那么，人才的未来在哪里？有很多因素会影响我们充分挖掘人才的办法。例如，科技和立法会把弹性工作制提上日程。全球性挑战和环境挑战会影响员工，他们可能不再会用传统的方式来工作。

我在结语想说的是，在你摸索自己和手头的人才共事的方式时，你需要灵活变通，反应及时。你希望他们怎么工作，什么时候工作，在哪儿工作，甚至是分配给他们什么任务，这些都要灵活一些。

记住：

• 多样化本身就在不断变化，改变本身会拓宽你的视角，因为你从差异中学到了东西

• 灵活变通会鼓励员工做出更多的探索，视角焕然一新

• 放松是激发创意的最佳办法之一（想想你沐浴或运动时是多么思绪万千吧！）

我希望这本书激发了你的一些创意，让你以不同的方法行事。

祝你好运！

# 值得一读的书

伟大的人才管理者很多，书自然也一样多。
以下是我喜欢的几本：

*Winning: Motivation for Business, Sport & Life*, Frank Dick, OBE, Abingdon Pub, 1992

*Coaching for Performance*, Sir John Whitmore, Nicholas Brealey, 2002

*Grow your own Leaders*, William C Byham, Audrey B Smith & Matthew J Paese, Financial Times Prentice Hall, 2002

*The Leadership Pipeline*, Ram Charan, Stephen J Drotter & James L Noel, Jossey-Bass, 2001

*29 Leadership Secrets from Jack Welch*, Robert Slater, McGraw-Hill, 2003

*The War for Talent*, Ed Michaels, Helen Handfield-Jones & Beth Axelrod, Harvard Business School Press, 2001

*The War for Talent: Getting the best from the best*, Michael R Williams, Institute of Personnel and Development, 2000

*Teambuilding Activities Pocketbook*, Paul Tizzard, Management Pocketbooks, 2006

*Mind Games: Inspirational Lessons from the World's Finest Sports Stars*, Jeff Grout & Sarah Perrin, Capstone, 2006

## 作者简介

### 安迪·克洛斯

安迪是维珍航空公司（Virgin Atlantic）组织和人员发展部的领头人。在金融服务、客户服务和咨询方面有丰富的工作经验，安迪热爱和他人分享自己的想法，也热衷于帮助员工、团队和机构提升业绩。

安迪把他对人才培养的热情拓展到了对家庭和运动的热爱上——尽力跟上孩子的步调，帮助几位从球员转行来的教练放缓过渡的步伐。

### 联系方式

你可以通过维珍航空公司联系安迪，或发邮件至 andycross@ntlworld.com

83 Somerset Road

Meadvale

Reigate

RH1 6ND

01737 224326

# 英汉对照管理丛书

1 办公室政治
2 身体语言
3 管理上司
4 做个学习者
5 做个好教练

6 战略管理
7 市场营销
8 管理模型
9 心理测试
10 人才管理

# 英汉对照管理袖珍手册

1 思维技巧
2 提高效率
3 时间管理
4 团队合作
5 激励
6 决策
7 会议事务
8 个人成功
9 人员管理
10 缓解紧张
11 资产负债表
12 现金流管理
13 预算管理
14 面谈高手
15 做个培训者
16 新员工培训
17 绩效管理

18 商务计划
19 管理变革
20 做个管理者
21 项目管理
22 评估管理
23 影响力
24 问题行为
25 商务演讲
26 客户服务
27 客户关系管理
28 电子商务
29 情感智商
30 谈判高手
31 问题解决方案
32 自我设计
33 电话语言
34 职业转型

35 管理初步
36 自信力
37 沟通高手
38 跨文化礼仪
39 健康导师
40 自我形象管理
41 领导力
42 人际网络
43 质量管理
44 冲突管理
45 授权管理
46 创意经理人
47 卓越销售
48 提高利润率
49 语音技巧
50 电子客户关怀